D0057901

Everyday Etiquette

PATRICIA ROSSI

Illustrations by Rob Barge

Everyday Etiquette

How to Navigate 101 Common and Uncommon Social Situations

St. Martin's Griffin
New York

FOR MY PRINCE, BOBBY:

Thank you for the love, laughter, and for being even more than you had promised. This life we're building together goes beyond my wildest dreams.

TO OUR PRECIOUS CUBS, JACKSON AND HARRISON:

Ron Howard said it best: "You must never at any point in your life ignore the possibility of something extraordinary coming along." Thanks for filling our hearts with "extraordinary," every single day!

EVERYDAY ETIQUETTE. Copyright © 2011 by Patricia Rossi. All rights reserved. Printed in the United States of America. For information, address St. Martin's Press, 175 Fifth Avenue, New York, N.Y. 10010.

www.stmartins.com

Design by Susan Walsh

ISBN 978-0-312-60427-1

First Edition: September 2011

10 9 8 7 6 5 4 3 2 1

Contents

Acknowledgments

First and foremost, I want to thank God for being way down the road ahead of me.

I am thankful for Tom and Yvonne Cronin: for believing in me.

Elizabeth Beier: for line-editing the book. Whew, you know how to make words sing! The way you do your job, honor those around you, and the sound of your laugh is beauty in motion to me.

Michelle Richter: Thank you for being a smart and feisty editor, comedian, and drill sergeant. You give it your all—more than a person could hope for. Thanks for always picking up on the second ring.

Steve Cohen: The boys want to take you to school for show-and-tell. Thank you for the opportunity to ride out my dream through St. Martin's. What an honor.

I also appreciate all of the cast and crew at St. Martin's: Meg Drislane, Joseph Goldschein, Nadea Mina, and Danielle Fiorella.

Thanks to my wonderful literary agents, Tricia Davey and Beth Gilliland.

Rob Barge: World's best artist and humanitarian—thanks for making me shine!

NBC Daytime: Larry Cotton, Cindi Edwards, Maureen Famiano, Deanna George, Lindsay MacDonald, Dave Nemeth, Rob Schweitzer, and April Wilson. Thank you for taking me under your wing, and for all the lessons and laughter on the show.

Jeff Houck: Thank you for being my trusted friend and editor at *The Tampa Tribune,* but I'm still afraid of that mood ring you wear.

Kathy Zader, Nina Stanley, Dr. Mollie Marti, Dr. Daisy Sutherland, Michelle Cook-Kaufmann, and Aaron Foster: Thanks for your way with words—they have given me wings.

My gratitude to: The Capital Grille, Dawn and Jim Rainwater, Vanessa Malson, John Wallace, and Chef James Shields for being the best!

A very special thanks to the *Tampa Tribune*, for allowing me to use content from my previously published articles; to Dabney Porte, for the social media information; to Melissa Galt, for your expert social media advice for the book; and Bob Burg, for your input on the how-to-say-no section of this book. Your help was invaluable.

To all my Myrnas: Jodi Avery, Wendi Braswell, Chris Davis, Jodi Gatti, Suzi Johnson, Sylvia Karalis, Sandi McKenna, Diane Philips, and Melissa Vardas. Thank you for making me a better person, friend, and mother. I cherish all of you.

Thanks to my two sisters, Dee Akhavein and Joy Barnes: You have been my best teachers.

Thank you to my parents, Neil and the late Miriam Barnes, and to Bob and Marie Rossi and all my family in NY, NC, and FL.

Lastly, thank you to the late Fred Long: You made my life a good life.

Test Your Etiquette IQ

1. *The proper place to wear a name tag?*

    A. On the left shoulder.
    B. On the right shoulder.
    C. On the left side near your waist.

2. *When using one of the six global handshakes, which one is the best choice?*

    A. The limp fish.
    B. The web-to-web, two to three pumps.
    C. The double handshake, four to five pumps.

3. *In the business arena*

    A. Only women stand for introductions and handshakes.
    B. Only men stand for introductions and handshakes.
    C. Both women and men stand for introductions and handshakes.

4. *Successful mingling at networking situations dictates that you*

    A. Go straight to the bar and buffet.

    B. Stand tall and proud in the middle of the room and hope people introduce themselves.

    C. Introduce yourself to one person or a group of three or more people.

5. *When inviting guests to lunch, is it proper protocol to ask where they would like to eat?*

    A. Giving them the choice shows respect and also insures that they will enjoy the meal.

    B. It puts too much pressure on the guests for them to decide how formal or informal.

    C. You are the host; you choose a restaurant that you know and trust.

6. **When male and female business colleagues arrive at a door, who opens the door?**

   A. The woman waits for the man to open the door.

   B. The man waits for the woman to open the door.

   C. Whoever is closest or arrives first opens the door.

7. **The easiest way to help your child make confident eye contact is to**

   A. Bribe them with candy.

   B. Have them look for the color of people's eyes as they say hello.

   C. Have them wear sunglasses so it isn't so intimidating.

8. **Is it acceptable to reply to voice-mail messages with an e-mail or a text?**

   A. If you prefer texting, then it is okay to respond to a voice mail with a text.

   B. If e-mailing will be faster and easier, then sending an e-mail is fine.

   C. The best option in replying is to follow the form of communication that the sender initiated.

9. **In social and business networking situations, it is important to stand straight because, when you lean, you lose**

   A. 50 percent of your credibility.

   B. 10 percent of your credibility.

   C. 90 percent of your credibility.

10. **Soft social skills are**

   A. How loud or soft we talk.

   B. Personal conduct codes that convey successful, professional, trustworthy, and corporative traits.

   C. When we wink or wave or give the thumbs-up sign.

11. **We make a first and lasting impression within**

    A. The first thirty seconds of meeting someone.

    B. One to three seconds of meeting someone.

    C. Five to seven seconds of meeting someone.

12. **If you are invited to a dinner party, the best gift to take to the host is**

    A. A music CD or picture frame.

    B. Flowers or wine.

    C. Coasters or chocolates.

13. **If your family is invited to a friend's house, is it okay to take your dog along?**

    A. No, as people might be allergic.

    B. Yes, your pet is part of the family.

    C. Only if it is a special holiday.

14. **When attending a tennis match, is it okay to scream and cheer?**

    A. Yes, if it's for your favorite player.

    B. No, you only scream and cheer at the end.

    C. No, loud noises distract the concentration of the players.

15. **If invited to a private box at a sporting event, you**

    A. Take the best seat in the suite; after all, you are the guest.

    B. Ask the hosts where they would like you to sit.

    C. Invite all your friends to the private suite.

ANSWERS

1. B 2. B 3. C 4. C 5. B & C 6. C 7. B 8. C 9. C 10. B 11. C

12. A & C 13. A 14. C 15. B

INTRODUCTION

For more than twenty years, I have helped people feel more confident and at ease in their everyday lives by teaching them about etiquette, protocol, and soft social skills. Whether I'm doing one-on-one coaching or group classes, writing blogs, visiting the White House, or appearing in my nationally syndicated "Manners Minute" television segments, I always focus on the same core principles: kindness as opposed to formality, and relationships as opposed to rules.

I grew up in the small mill town of Bessemer City, North Carolina. I was a tomboy who spent most of my childhood climbing trees, outrunning the boys, and usually covered in mud. Despite these rambunctious addictions, I found myself enchanted by the Southern graces taught to me by the female matriarchs in my family and community.

Bessemer City certainly wasn't Charleston or Savannah. It wasn't even Charlotte, which was about an hour to the east of us, but seemed like a world away.

I can remember one spring day when, perched on the branch of a tall pine tree, slingshot in hand, I was stopped in my tracks at the sight of my mother down below in the driveway in a beautiful flowing gown getting into the car with my dad as they headed to the Annual Heart Ball in Charlotte.

Not long after that vision, I retired my BB gun, borrowed my grandmother's tea set, and started hosting tea parties for the neighborhood kids and their pets. The funny part was, because of a shortage of young girls on East Tennessee Avenue back in the seventies, my party guests usually consisted of the boys in the surrounding houses attending against their will in fear that I'd beat them up if they didn't come!

Yearning for art, music, and culture, I headed for college in Florida the fall after graduating high school. A few years later I was spending summers in Europe while earning college credit. I was a sponge for all the glorious gifts I would discover and the unforgettable people I would meet from all different cultures and backgrounds.

Observing scholars and dropouts, rich and poor, famous painters and starving artists, I witnessed how social skills played such an important role in life and how they propelled some to great success, while others were held back by the lack of them.

I hope this book helps propel you to great success, by being the very best that you can be.

One

INTRODUCING YOURSELF

What I Learned in the White House

In the late nineties, my husband and I were fortunate to be invited to the White House for a special event in the Oval Office. With fewer than one hundred guests, it was an annual celebration for Italian Americans and featured many famous actors, singers, writers, sports figures, and politicians. As I gazed around the ornate room and explored its vintage artwork and décor, I knew the historic mansion offered so much more to explore.

I walked over to the security woman who had checked us in earlier. I was about to ask her a question when she said, "Ma'am, I want to thank you because you are the only person who spoke to me and asked me how my night was going when I was checking you in for the party." I thought, *I've got to say something funny,* so I said, in my best Southern drawl, "I'm tired of being in there with all those stuffy people [not really]. Is there anything else you can show this girl from Bessemer City, North Carolina, that's interesting and historical?" She immediately smiled, ripped the walkie-talkie from her belt, and said into it, "I'm bringing a guest with me to the such-and-such room."

We ventured down several long corridors until we ended up in a large, beautiful office, a magnificent space. My eyes immediately fell upon the large wooden desk that anchored the room. I had seen this wonderful image in so many photographs through the years. Little John-John Kennedy had hid under and peeked out of this desk in his father's office. I asked the security guard if I could please just touch it. The guard leaned toward me and whispered, "You wanna see something really cool?" She opened the drawer of the desk and pointed out a crude hole about four inches across. It looked as if it had been dug out with a dull screwdriver blade. Historians believe this hole housed the concealed tape recorder during some Watergate conversations; not very high-tech. It gave me chills. I asked the guard if I could go back and get my husband. I didn't want him to miss a chance to see this piece of history. As we walked back to the party to get him, I realized that the *simple* act of being kind and acknowledging another human being had granted me favor in the White House.

It's so important to address and respect other people in each and every situation. Other people matter. That's the lesson I learned in the hallowed halls of the White House.

Have you ever been introduced to someone who wouldn't look you in the eye? Or someone who shook your hand as if you had some sort of contagious disease? When you walked away from those encounters, how did you feel?

If you didn't feel good, you're not alone.

People want to feel that they matter. They want to be known, respected, and remembered. The better you are at making people feel that way, the more likely you are to make a good first impression.

Making people feel acknowledged is not a gift that you have to be born with. It's a skill that can be learned. You don't have to be an extrovert or even a people person to make a favorable first impression. Just review the simple techniques described in this chapter and practice using them as often as you can. Eventually they will become second nature and will easily be incorporated into your everyday life and interactions.

Just a few small changes in how you act can make a big difference.

THE APPROACH

When you're approaching someone to introduce yourself, walk up, extend your right hand, look the person in the eye, and say, "Hello, I'm _____." It's that simple.

Extending your hand first demonstrates self-confidence and openness, traits that make you seem both likable and competent. Technically, when it comes to workplace introductions, the higher-up should be the first to extend his or her hand. As a practical matter, however, you shouldn't wait too long. If the other person (even the company CEO!) doesn't take the lead, just get your hand out there to avoid an awkward pause. Maybe even the CEO needs a lesson in etiquette!

PROPER INTRODUCTIONS

Making a proper introduction helps enhance your business sense and can boost your self-confidence. It also demonstrates your insight and respect for others. Remember the old saying: "You never get a second chance to make a good first impression."

Here are some guidelines to follow for a poised and professional image when making introductions.

+ Introduce people in business according to rank, not gender or age. Example: "Dr. Mollie Marti, I would like you to meet Dr. Tom Hanson."
+ Be sure to look at the people you are introducing, starting with the person of greatest importance.
+ Clearly state each person's name to demonstrate professionalism and credibility. Try to provide a bit of information along with their names, as this can serve as a conversation starter.
+ If introducing people of equal rank, start with the older person.
+ In business, the client, guest, or visitor outranks the boss or coworker and should be introduced first.

- When introducing someone to a family member, you should typically say the other person's name first.
- In a social situation, men are generally introduced to women. Example: "Melissa, I'd like to introduce Bobby."

BODY LANGUAGE

With communication in person, body language is even more important than your words. The way you walk, stand, and move tells people a lot about you, whether you're aware of it or not. Every thought or feeling you have about yourself is telegraphed in your body language.

Think about the last party or networking event you attended. How did you decide whom to approach? What helped you figure out whether a particular person was someone you wanted to meet?

Chances are, you observed people's movements, their gestures, and their posture—all of those nonverbal cues we rely on to help us make quick decisions in social situations. At the same time, other people were making similar observations about you. What do you think your body language was telling them?

Here are six simple things you can do to convey both self-confidence and respect for others without saying a word.

- Stand up straight. When introducing yourself, stand up straight with your shoulders facing the other person. Standing tall and proud sends the message that you are confident, trustworthy, and vibrant, whereas slouching indicates that you're unsure of yourself and uncomfortable with your surroundings.
- Don't lean on anything. When you lean, you lose 90 percent of your credibility.
- Place your feet about six to eight inches apart, with one foot slightly in front of the other. This will naturally improve your posture and make you feel steadier on your feet. Your toes should be facing the other person to avoid sending a silent signal that you want to get away. (Be aware that when

you are speaking with someone and their torso and feet are not facing you, it usually means they want to get away.)

+ Stand approximately three feet away from whomever you're speaking with. If you stand too close, you're invading the other person's personal space (remember the "Close Talker" on *Seinfeld*?). On the other hand, if you stand too far away, you may make the other person feel as though you don't really want to be near them.

+ Make eye contact. It shows that you respect yourself and the other person, that you're giving your full attention to the person in front of you. If you're shy or have trouble making eye contact, try to focus on the color of the other person's eyes. If it helps you, pretend that it's your job to find out their eye color. You can also try looking at the person's forehead, right between their eyes.

+ Smile! A smile is contagious and will immediately put the other person at ease. Be careful not to overdo smiling in a professional setting, however, since you don't want to be perceived as frivolous or unintelligent.

+ Don't look over another person's shoulder or around the room. This will make you look easily distracted, or make the other person feel that you are not interested in what they are saying.

WHAT TO SAY

When introducing yourself in a business arena, always state your first and last name along with your title, remembering to say the client's name first. Example: "Hello, Ms. Goodwin. I'm Kelli Hadd, national VP of sales and training."

THE HANDSHAKE

A handshake is the only physical contact you're likely to have with someone you've just met, so it's important to get it right. Fortunately, a good handshake isn't complicated.

THE CONFIDENT
"WEB-TO-WEB"
3-PUMP HANDSHAKE

"QUEEN'S SHAKE"
TOO ARROGANT

"BONE CRUSHER"
TOO PAINFUL

"FIST BUMP"
TOO CASUAL

The correct way to initiate a handshake is to extend your right arm toward the other person with your right thumb pointing up.

Your hands should connect "web to web" (the web is the portion of your hand between your thumb and forefinger).

The connection should be snug, but not uncomfortable, and should be followed by three up-and-down pumps. If the handshake goes beyond three pumps, let the other person end the shake when they want to. As long as the other person is still pumping, it's important not to yank your hand away even if the other person's hand is sweaty. Pulling your hand away before the other person is ready will come across as a rejection, and nobody likes to feel rejected.

If you try to initiate a handshake, but the other person doesn't respond, don't worry about it. Stay relaxed, lower your hand, maintain eye contact, and continue talking.

Never shake hands while in a seated or subservient position. Stand up, then shake hands; this applies to women as well. If a barrier is between you and the other person, such as a desk or table, then come around from behind the barrier for the handshake, never lean across it.

Although a good handshake is simple, you can easily make a small mistake that conveys a bad impression. Here are a few types of handshakes you should avoid at all costs.

- The *limp fish*. This is when your hand is limp and feels to the other person as if it has no bones (not a good feeling). Rather than grasping the other person's hand, you're making him or her do all the work. This type of handshake says to the other person, "I'm weak; I don't believe in myself; I'm not a winner." To avoid a limp fish handshake, grasp the other person's hand firmly and maintain a snug connection. If someone gives you a limp fish, try to push your hand in a little closer to get a better connection.
- The *bone crusher*. The bone crusher is the opposite of the limp fish handshake. It's when you squeeze the other person's hand so firmly that it causes pain or discomfort. This type of handshake tells people that you're anxious and need to dominate others to feel powerful.
- The *queen's shake*. This is when you hold on to someone's fingertips, instead of making palm-to-palm contact. This type of handshake makes other people feel that you don't want to touch them and conveys an "I'm better than you" attitude.
- The *wrestler*. The wrestler handshake is when you turn the other person's hand over so that your hand is on top. It is an aggressive and blatant show of power. If someone uses a wrestler shake with you, correct it by taking a two-inch step to the left while gradually returning your hand to a vertical position. This will help restore the balance of power.

- The *double handshake*. This is when you use two hands. Your right hand grasps the other person's as in a correct handshake, but your left hand is placed on top of theirs. This handshake should only be used in intimate situations, such as to convey condolences. It tells the other person that you're feeling for them, but if used in the wrong situation, it feels insincere and inappropriate.
- The *fist bump*. This is technically a handshake substitute rather than a type of handshake, but President Barack Obama's use of it has made it acceptable in certain situations. It is most appropriate when used by close friends as a celebratory or congratulatory gesture, so don't try it at your next board meeting, unless the CEO initiates it.

Some germaphobes have begun using the fist bump to avoid handshakes; they believe it to be more sanitary. Since you never know if this is what's going on, if someone initiates a fist bump with you, just go along with it. However, since it is still not generally accepted as an appropriate substitute for a handshake, I recommend against initiating a fist bump in most situations.

One last little tip: if you tend to have sweaty hands, use cornstarch or powder or spray antiperspirant on your hands before social events. This will help keep your palms dry so you can shake hands with confidence.

Also, modern etiquette dictates that in social situations a man or a woman can initiate a handshake. It is no longer customary for an elderly woman to initiate a handshake with a younger woman or a gentleman with a lady. Be mindful, with elderly men or women, it might be wise to pause and let them reach out, as they may have arthritis.

In business, the higher-ranked person should extend their hand, but if they don't, it is wise to go ahead and initiate the handshake.

Two

COMMUNICATING WITH CONFIDENCE

The Lost Opportunity

I was visiting a Fortune 500 hiring manager whose office was spotless and decorated in clean, minimalist modern motifs. He was impeccably dressed, all the way down to his bow tie, and his speech and grammar matched his title, dress, and office décor. He was conducting a series of interviews that I was sitting in on as an observer.

In between the interviews, the manager made phone calls to invite other candidates to come in and interview in person. I asked why he was making the calls rather than someone in his personnel department. He replied that you can tell a lot about a person by the way they start, continue, and end a phone call. He put his phone on speaker and dialed a number from one of the résumés on his desk. After the second ring, a loud, booming, techno-funk beat blared out. After about ten seconds of this ear-bleeding mess a man's screaming voice came on the recorder and said, "What's up?" The hiring manager paused, hung up the phone, and without missing a beat said, "The unemployment line."

It's important that all levels of your communication present a professional persona. That candidate's résumé looked amazing: he had graduated with honors from an Ivy League school and had interned at a prestigious Fortune 500 company. Two words accompanied by a loud techno-beat blast on his voice mail ruined his chance at a near-impossible-to-land job interview. Make sure all personal written and audio information, as well as that shared on social networks such as Facebook and Twitter, is professional.

Confidence is fueled by knowledge. When you know how to do something correctly, you feel much more confident doing it. When you feel confident, people feel more comfortable around you, and communication becomes a lot easier. That's why this chapter is so important, especially if you often feel awkward in social situations.

This chapter may seem to offer a lot of rules to follow, but don't get discouraged if you find it hard to remember every single one. As long as you are kind, considerate, and respectful toward others, you can't go wrong.

CELL PHONES

Cell phones are wonderfully useful, but when used inappropriately, they can be a source of embarrassment or annoyance. They

distract you from what's going on in front of you, and when you're distracted, it can be perceived as a lack of consideration toward others.

It's important to be fully present when you're speaking to someone. In a face-to-face conversation or in a meeting, people know when you're trying to sneak a peek at your phone. You're not a secret agent. There's only one 007—and I'm afraid it's not you or me. If you're in a meeting, keep your cell phone out of sight and out of mind. Let calls go to voice mail and check your messages later.

If you're going into a meeting and you might get an urgent phone call, let the other attendees know in advance: "I may have to leave the meeting to take an important call I'm expecting." Don't let this become a habit; these types of urgent calls should be few and far between.

Here are a few other tips for respectful cell phone use.

+ Stay calm. Overly emotional cell phone conversations are awkward for the people around you. If you find yourself getting angry or upset, try to end the conversation and call the person back when you're alone.
+ Do not "cell yell." Why is it that as soon as we're talking on a cell phone, we think the person we're talking to is stone-deaf? Use your normal speaking voice.
+ Never put your cell phone on the table. Whether at a restaurant, a board meeting, or at home, cell phones should never be part of your place setting.
+ Keep your phone quiet at public events. When you go to the movies, a play, sports events, or any other event, turn your ringer off or use the vibrate function.
+ Observe the ten-foot rule. When talking on a cell phone, you should maintain a distance of at least ten feet from the person nearest you. It doesn't matter how softly you speak, if you are standing too close to someone, that person has no choice but to listen to your personal business. If you are expecting an important phone call in a public setting, ask

permission to take the call, doing your best to keep it brief and out of proximity of others.

✦ Love the one you're with. When you are on a date or at a social engagement with others, don't take cell phone calls. Furthermore, it is not polite to take a call in the middle of a conversation. Let calls go to voice mail and return them later.

✦ If you are driving now, you should talk later. Sometimes multitasking is not a good idea. Proof of this is that accidents have increased due to the use of cell phones while driving; even if you use a hands-free device, you are still distracted. Your calls can wait until you have arrived at your destination. If the call is important and you cannot wait, pull your car over, park, and then make or accept your call.

Cell phone etiquette is just a matter of being considerate of others.

E-MAIL

The first thing you should keep in mind about e-mail is that once you hit Send, there's no going back. If you're stressed or upset when typing an e-mail, wait twenty-four hours and then reread the message before you send it.

Everything you send out in digital form (e-mails, blog posts, tweets, Facebook status updates, photographs, and videos) is all part of your "digital footprint." Keep your digital footprint clean since you never know who will see it. Never post or send an e-mail that you would not want your boss, grandmother, or a blind date to see. When it comes to the Internet and digital/viral media, there are no do-overs. What's done is done, and what's out there is out there. Forever. Never forget that.

Here are a few more e-mail etiquette tips.

✦ Keep e-mails brief. How's your in-box looking these days? Full, right? So is everyone else's. Don't make people read a dissertation in an e-mail message, because they probably won't.

+ Use proper spelling and grammar. Just because it's an e-mail doesn't mean you should throw proper English out the window. Read your message carefully before hitting Send to catch any errors.

+ Don't write in all CAPS. It's like shouting at the person who opens your e-mail.

+ Make sure you don't hit Reply All when you mean to hit Reply. This is one of the biggest e-mail blunders people make and can lead to serious consequences, especially in the workplace.

+ Don't put anything too personal in an e-mail. Remember that e-mail messages are easily forwarded, printed, and shared and can be saved forever.

+ Use bcc. For everyone's privacy, when you're sending a message to a group of people, use the bcc (blind carbon copy) function, so the recipients can't see one another's e-mail address.

+ Use a subject line that tells the recipient what your e-mail is about. If your entire message is contained in the subject line, use *eom* (end of message) so the recipient knows she doesn't have to open the e-mail. For example: "Subject: See you at lunch today! (eom)"

+ Please and thank you. It is a good idea to read your e-mail out loud to be certain the tone is what you intend it to be. The use of the words *please* and *thank you* go a long way.

+ Never assume the intent of another person's e-mail to you. If you are not sure of the person's objective, you should ask to avoid unnecessary misunderstandings.

Remember, e-mail is only one means of communication. Don't use it as a tool to avoid in-person or telephone conversations.

NEVER TEXT IN **ALL CAPS.** IT'S LIKE SHOUTING AT SOMEONE.

IF YOUR MESSAGE IS URGENT, USE THE PHONE.

NEVER TEXT WHILE DRIVING. IT'S EXTREMELY DANGEROUS.

TEXT MESSAGING

Texting is great for sending short messages, especially when you're in a quiet environment and can't use your phone. Unfortunately, some of us have gotten so used to texting that we have forgotten it's not our only option!

Remember that text messaging is not a replacement for in-person or even telephone conversations, and that relationships are not built on text messages. It's also important to follow these texting rules:

- ✦ Never text while driving. It's extremely dangerous.
- ✦ Never text (or read text messages) while you are in a meeting or talking to someone face-to-face. It tells people that you don't care about what they have to say.

- Never text in all CAPS. It's like shouting at someone.
- Think about how the recipient will "hear" your message. In some cases, because the recipient can't hear the tone of your voice, your words may be received quite differently from how you intended.
- Never use text messaging to deliver important or upsetting news. Some things require an in-person conversation.
- Never assume. Finally, don't assume that everyone can receive text messages or knows how to access them. Some people simply don't use text messaging. If something is urgent, pick up the phone and call.

MAKING CONVERSATION

Conversation is meant to be a back-and-forth exchange between two people. It's not a lecture, a speech, or an interview. Here are a few tips to keep conversation flowing.

- Try to get the other person to talk as much as possible. Asking open-ended questions (such as "What are your travel plans this summer?") instead of yes/no questions (such as "Are you going on vacation?") is a great start.
- When the other person is talking, pay attention! This may sound simple, but it's easy to forget when your smartphone is buzzing.
- Never ask someone "What do you do?" Especially during difficult economic times—periods of layoffs, restructuring, downsizing, etc.—this question could turn out to be an awkward conversation stopper. Instead, ask something like "How do you like to spend your free time?"
- If someone asks you what you do for a living, don't give a one-word answer. If you're a consultant, for example, you might say, "I help small-business owners learn how to increase their revenue while decreasing their working hours."
- Demonstrate that you're paying attention to what the other person is saying. Maintain eye contact, nod when

appropriate, and occasionally repeat what the other person says (a technique called mirroring). It means a lot to people when they know you're focused on them.

✦ Listen. When someone asks you a question, make sure to listen to the entire question before answering. Otherwise you may end up giving an unresponsive or inappropriate answer. If someone asks you a question you don't want to answer, try answering the question with another question. You can also try using humor and changing the subject. For example, if someone asks, "Who are you voting for for president?" instead of answering, you could say, "I've been so busy lately, I can't even vote on what to have for dinner. Do you know of any great restaurants?"

✦ Say the other person's name. It's simple to do, but meaningful. People love hearing their own name because they want to feel known and be remembered, but don't overdo it.

Every once in a while, you'll run into people who want to tell you things you don't really want to know. They might give you all the details of their latest medical problem, specific information about what they found last night in their baby's diaper, or the latest update on their ex-spouse's financial situation. In other words, TMI.

When this happens to you, do not ask any follow-up questions, even if it seems like the only possible response. As soon as you ask even a single question, you're inviting the other person to continue—ad nauseam—with their inappropriate revelations. Instead, offer a short response, then steer the conversation in a new direction.

In the case of the parent with diaper details, for example, you could try something like "Sounds like you could use a vacation! When was the last time you were able to get away?" Hopefully the conversation will turn to their latest trip, and you won't have to hear anything more about baby's bottom.

NAME GAME

What if you can't remember the name of the person you're speaking with?

Whatever you do, never say "I forgot your name" or "I can't remember your name." Those kinds of statements will just make the other person feel bad, and they're unnecessary. Instead, say something like "Your name is right on the tip of my tongue" or "It's been such a long day, could you please tell me your name again?"

Of course, you'll make an even better impression if you can remember the person's name in the first place. If you have trouble remembering names, here are a few techniques to try.

- ✦ **Listen.** Really listen when someone is telling you his or her name. Sometimes instead of listening, we're thinking about what to say next. Don't do this. Listen to the person's name and repeat it back as soon as possible: "It's so nice to meet you, Jackson."
- ✦ **Repeat.** After meeting someone new, say the person's name a few times to imprint it in your memory. Use it while speaking to the person, but not so frequently that it feels strange.
- ✦ **Nickname.** Give the person a nickname that helps you remember them (Tall Timothy, for example). If you use this technique, make sure you don't say the nickname out loud. Keep it to yourself!
- ✦ **Write it down.** After you meet someone and go your separate ways, remember to key in and save in your smartphone or computer the person's name, where you met them, and something that will remind you of what you discussed. This is especially helpful at networking events.
- ✦ **Spelling.** If a person has an unusual name or the name has more than one spelling, ask them how they spell it. If a name is generally spelled only one way, such as Robert or David, you could ask if they prefer Bob or Dave. Never shorten a person's name unless they have suggested you do

so—for instance, by calling a woman Pat after she has stated her name is Patricia.

+ **Repetition.** When someone tells you their name, say it and spell it three times to yourself.
+ **Change focus.** Sometimes we forget someone's name because we are feeling socially self-conscious. Our focus is on whether *we* are looking, speaking, or acting acceptably. Turn your focus to the other person and on putting them at ease, and it will be much easier to recall their name.
+ **Reintroduce yourself.** If you see someone you haven't seen in a long time, reintroduce yourself. This may prompt them to tell you their name as well.
+ **You're brilliant!** When someone remembers your name and you just cannot remember theirs, try saying, "Wow, you have an amazing memory! Please tell me your name again; it's been a very long day."

POLITELY ENDING A CONVERSATION

From time to time you will encounter a "conversational rambler." Someone has you in their clutches and won't stop talking. To get away without being rude, start by saying something positive, such as "I'm so happy I got to talk to you." Follow up with a brief explanation of why you have to go: "I see someone else I have to speak to" or "I really should go say hello to the host before she disowns me!" Then simply smile and excuse yourself.

Following are more examples of ways to politely end a conversation:

+ **Long-winded friend on the phone.** "Can I call you later? I have some things to finish up and I'd better get busy."
+ **Stranger strikes up a conversation.** Chances are you looked approachable. A positive way to end the conversation is to say, "It was nice talking with you, but I have to run. Have a good day!"

- ✦ **Coworker.** "Wow, you sure did a great job on that project!" Then quickly add, "And now I really have to get back to work." If you need to interact with this person to accomplish a task, request a meeting: "This is something that deserves more than a passing conversation. Would you please e-mail me some times when we can meet to resolve this efficiently?"
- ✦ **Boring relative.** "I'm so glad to hear about [whatever the relative has been talking about], but I had better go check in on [elderly relative/baby/children/spouse/parent]. It's been great talking with you!"
- ✦ **Friendly drunk.** Proximity breeds conversation. You will want to move away after saying, "Well, have a good evening."

Some people seem to have an uncanny ability to structure their conversations to make it difficult to get out of them. Something about the way they drag out their stories makes escape nearly impossible. This is known as the "can't get a word in edgewise" dilemma.

If caught on the horns of that dilemma, you just have to make that uncomfortable leap and end the conversation. The best way is to begin with a simple apology, then follow with an explanation of why you must go. "Hey, I'm really sorry. I know you have much more you want to tell me, but I'm running late for an appointment and I have to get going. Can we pick this up at a later date?"

Kindness is always imperative!

RESPONDING TO GOSSIP

Etiquette is about relationships, not rules. But I firmly believe in one rule: *Never gossip.* We've all done it, but that doesn't make it right. If you can kick the habit, you'll feel much better about yourself. Try to form a new habit, such as spreading good news or information about other people.

It can be difficult to refrain from gossiping, especially when you have a juicy bit of news about someone that would be of interest to others. You should still do your best to resist the urge. Remember, gossiping may get you attention, but that attention is fleeting. What lasts is your reputation as someone who cannot be trusted with confidential or personal information.

Even if you don't initiate gossip yourself, you will inevitably encounter someone who does. When that happens, you have a few options:

+ You can try to change the subject by saying something neutral and positive, such as "What a beautiful sweater! Where did you get it?"
+ You could tell the other person that you're not comfortable talking about people when they're not there to defend themselves.
+ Or try using my favorite response to gossip: "Oh, Lord, I have way too much to fix in myself before I use my time and energy talking about other people."

Three

SOCIAL MEDIA IN MODERN TIMES

How Social Media Made Secret Wishes Come True

In 2008, my friend Sandra McKenna @McMedia introduced me to the amazing world of social media as a great way to engage in business and also personal life. I remember I rolled my eyes and thought to myself, *I don't have time to fit even one more thing into my busy schedule.* I soon learned that I didn't have time *not* to.

Sandra is a travel and food writer. I watched her interactions on Twitter and Facebook yield her not only great connections, but also free trips to Italy, Mexico, and other exciting destinations. She also landed interviews with major fashion designers and pop stars, and even had the good fortune to test-drive an Indy pace car. She soon became the writer and producer for the popular *Midlife Road Trip* show and has secured her dream job and now travels with a film crew all over the world, all because she connected with people via Twitter and Facebook. This is Sandra's advice:

"You have to be sincere, be yourself. People want to engage with real people. Using social media for business or for casual conversation is no different from the 'old-fashioned way' of meeting at a mixer. It's based on building trusted relationships." People were attracted to Sandra's sense of humor, her enthusiasm, her kindness, and her interest in them. Her persona online is the same as it is in real life.

Sandi was able to reach out to like-minded people and engage them in meaningful conversation. She took the time to share information with others and reaped the rewards.

Social media Web sites such as Facebook, LinkedIn, and Twitter allow us to quickly share information about our lives with anyone and everyone. This can be a great way to keep in touch, but remember, there is no such thing as privacy when it comes to social media. Assume that everything you put on social media sites is permanent, searchable, and easily accessible for all time.

Before you post anything to a social media site (including photos, messages, links, etc.), ask yourself whether you would mind seeing it on the front page of your newspaper or AOL home page. If you wouldn't want to see it there, don't post it online.

There's no way to control what happens to your social media posts. Once they're made public, they're out there forever. Potential employers, future loved ones and their families, college admissions officers, and everyone else you know and don't know will be able to find and view every comment, post, and photo.

As with any communication, consideration and kindness are most important when it comes to social media.

- ✦ When using social media for business, remember that you have to build relationships before you try to sell your products. How would you feel if you were at a party, having a nice conversation, and someone just walked up and launched into a sales pitch? That's what it's like when you jump into social media and immediately start selling.
- ✦ On Facebook, don't tag other people in unflattering or off-the-wall photos. Tags are searchable, and you never know who will find them. If someone requests to be untagged, remove the tag as soon as possible.
- ✦ On Twitter, keep it real. Use a photo of yourself as your avatar (an avatar is an image that shows up next to your social media posts and tweets) and fill out the bio section. Use the same picture on all your social media sites for professionalism and continuity.

Don't use your Twitter and Facebook stream exclusively to promote yourself, or you will quickly become boring and others will "unfollow" you. The same thing goes for using direct messages to spam other users; it's not nice and it will cost you followers. Twitter and Facebook are about engaging other people, not pushing your sales message on anyone who will listen. Give and share interesting and useful information as frequently as possible.

FACEBOOK

Facebook has millions of active users and its numbers grow daily. It is one of the most visited Web sites in the world and is enjoyed by young and old. Many people have found that Facebook is a critical addition to their Web-working toolbox. It can be customized to be anything you want, from a way to keep in close contact with family and friends to an efficient professional tool for your business.

Below are some tips for navigating your way around Facebook.

- ✦ Make sure you have a presentable and updated profile. Use your real name and a current photo rather than a cartoon or graphic image. Be certain the picture is tasteful and neutral. Don't hold up an opinionated sign from the last political rally, or a foolhardy picture from your bachelorette party. Provide information about your work status, Web sites, blog, and e-mail. Be cautious about disclosing your real birth date or location, to protect against identity theft or the unlikely but frightening chance of stalkers. Customize your Facebook settings to limit what can be viewed by friends, family, coworkers, or employers.
- ✦ Provide value to your followers by sharing your hobbies, interesting information, pictures from trips, business news, and useful content.
- ✦ Be careful you don't post too many updates, such as "breathing in" and then the next second "breathing out." Lunch choices, weather reports, and depressing song lyrics will not add much value to your offerings, unless you are a food critic or songwriter.
- ✦ Don't be a cyberstalker. Avoid randomly friending people you don't know or posting on their walls. It sends a creepy message, and you could become known as a friend poacher. If you must friend a person you don't know, explain who you are in a direct message, why you are friending them, and how you know them. Example: "I'm your sister's college roommate." Or, better yet, have your roommate make the introduction by suggesting you as a friend on Facebook.
- ✦ Refrain from barging into someone's Facebook domain via instant chat. Don't assume your friends, family, and

business colleagues are open and free to chat just because you see them online. If they don't immediately respond, they probably stepped away from the computer, are busy with work, or have other obligations.

+ Avoid oversharing personal information and private emotions. It's Facebook, not *The Jerry Springer Show*. Keep your secrets, family skeletons, and grooming habits in the closet where they belong. Share them only with your closest friends.

+ A proper response time to wall posts and messages is within twenty-four hours. If you check Facebook infrequently, let your contacts know that you respond to e-mail faster than Facebook.

+ Don't alter the status of your relationship without first making that status change known to the other person. Before you do something in haste, think about all the people who will see what you post. Respect the feelings of others and refrain from embarrassing or hurtful actions.

+ Direct business colleagues to your LinkedIn social media site if they ask to be Facebook friends and only accept requests from friends and family. Giving people another choice to connect as opposed to not responding is a more polite approach.

TWITTER

The social networking site Twitter has many great uses. Besides using it to keep family and friends connected to your daily life, you can use it for professional purposes, such as advertising job openings, business networking, and sharing news briefs. Twitter offers a microblogging platform whose posts are called tweets. Tweets are short posts of up to 140 characters that are displayed on your profile page. Twitter can add value to your networking life depending on how well you use it.

- No tweeting if you are in a meeting, with a group of people, or one-on-one with another person. Give real people your full attention. People always know if you're tweeting under the table no matter how inconspicuous you think you are.
- If you see a great tweet, it's okay to retweet it. Just be sure to give the original tweeter credit on your Twitter feed for their 140 characters of brilliance. If someone retweets what you share, be sure to thank them.
- Consider it an honor when people follow you. They are saying they like the content you share, so follow them as a reciprocal courtesy. An exception to this rule is if people follow you only to hawk their snake oil. In that case, unfollow them.
- Never tweet in sacred situations, such as church services, weddings, funerals, baptisms, bar mitzvahs, etc.
- Before you post a tweet, picture it in skywriting across the heavens. Never tweet while upset, inebriated, or unhappy with your boss or company. What you put out there will linger forever in cyberspace, so be cautious about tweeting negative content.
- Be neat when you tweet. Use proper grammar, since your grammar and usage tells a story about you. There is more than one way to be seen and received, so be careful with too many abbreviations and acronyms. We don't want others to have to decipher our tweets. Keep in mind that sloppily written posts are like leaving the house with your shirt incorrectly buttoned and one shoe untied.
- Hashtags should only be used when relevant. A hashtag highlights and covers events that are happening in real time. They bring communities of people with similar interests together. Random hashtags are unnecessary noise.
- Refrain from using automation tools to connect or communicate with your followers. Real-time interaction is what makes Twitter an amazing tool. Genuine engagement

is the key ingredient in using social media, not a robotic automessage received in real time.

+ Use direct messaging for private conversations and keep in mind that you should never post highly personal information about yourself or others. If in question, pause and use the direct message option. You can always choose to post openly later, but if you make something public first, it's too late to go back and make it private. Remember, when in doubt, don't.

+ Be your very best on Twitter in everything you post. Be careful not to become too relaxed and share things that don't represent you well. Keep in mind that you never know who might be tracking your tweets.

LINKEDIN

Use LinkedIn to maintain a list of contacts you trust in business. These people are called connections. You may invite anyone to become a connection, even if he or she is not a site user. You can use this list of connections in many ways, such as finding jobs, professional people, and business opportunities. Employers can post jobs and seek out potential candidates. If you are searching for employment, you can review profiles of hiring managers and bookmark jobs that you would like to apply for.

Below are some tips to consider once you have decided to become a member of LinkedIn.

+ LinkedIn is part viral résumé and part sophisticated business card. It is a great way to market yourself, so take the time to set up everything professionally.

+ Your profile picture is worth a thousand words. At a glance your professional demeanor can quickly be summed up, so make sure your profile picture is current, well presented, and has a business feel. It could be a great investment to hire a professional photographer. Refrain from posting additional pictures, such as photos with children or at sporting events.

- Your bio is the second most important thing to fill out and post. Be truthful. Highlight all the areas in your career that could be of interest to a prospective hiring manager. Don't embellish or tell fairy tales or little white lies. They will come back to haunt you.
- Join groups on LinkedIn that are of interest and to which you can add value. For example, if you're a writer, you can join a writers' group.
- Make sure to update your profile daily, since it only takes ten seconds and keeps your LinkedIn silhouette fresh and current.
- Add worth to other LinkedIn pages by giving thoughtful and honest recommendations.
- Status updates should be of a professional nature. Save the more casual comments for Twitter or Facebook.
- Send your best wishes and congratulations when someone gets a new job or a promotion. Also, send congratulations for any favorable news in the press about a LinkedIn contact company.
- Respond to requests to be added within twenty-four hours.
- Be positive and never say anything unfavorable or negative about a former boss or company. First impressions last, so make sure everything you say is presented thoughtfully and positively. You never know who will read your posts and bio.
- Keep an eye on the status updates of others and maintain contact by responding and commenting.
- To build credibility, answer questions and also ask them. It's a wonderful way to profile your knowledge and build rapport with people.

SKYPE

Skype is an amazing tool for communication in business, and with friends and loved ones. How wonderful it is that grandparents can read a story, via Skype, to their grandchildren. Skype adds another dimension to connecting. It brings the interaction more up close and personal than an e-mail or phone call ever could.

Here are some great tips for Skype users.

+ Always instant-message or e-mail to make an appointment to talk via Skype. Never just call directly, as the recipient may prefer to e-mail or have a traditional phone chat.
+ Make sure you identify yourself at the beginning of the call. Never just launch into talking. Instead say, "Hello, this is [your name] calling. How are you today?" Then proceed with the conversation.
+ Make sure you and your surroundings are presentable. Remember that you, your clothing, and the background are the visual focus on Skype if you are using the video or webcam. Prepare your space for a professional encounter. Make sure pets, people, cell phones, and that velvet Elvis poster won't be distractions.
+ Resist the temptation to multitask. Sending a quick text or glancing over your snail mail may deter a successful Skype call. Give your full attention to whomever you are Skyping with.
+ Be sure to fill out your profile and also read the profiles of any new contacts you will be Skyping with.
+ Refrain from constantly looking down at yourself in the little video window. This is unprofessional and shows insecurity.
+ Keep your eyes in the vicinity of the lens. Practice if you have to. This makes you appear more presentable and video savvy.

YOUTUBE

YouTube is a free, interactive, worldwide Web site where people upload video clips of themselves, children, pets, their expertise, interests, hobbies, music, and business ventures.

Here are a few YouTube dos and don'ts.

✦ Do complete your profile. Use proper grammar and refrain from foul language.

✦ Do focus on adding value and good content. You can build a nice following on YouTube if this is your main focus.

✦ Don't ever post a video of someone else without first getting their permission.

✦ Don't falsely categorize your videos. If you are posting a comedy, don't label it "high-speed car chase" just to capture additional viewers.

✦ Offer positive feedback to the videos you enjoy by giving them your thumbs-up, video comments, or by leaving a favorable message in the comment box. Don't leave negative remarks or use profanity.

✦ Do provide caption options for deaf viewers.

✦ Don't subscribe to someone's YouTube channel just so the person will subscribe to yours.

✦ Don't stalk anyone with multiple requests to subscribe to your channel. People will subscribe on a single request if they want to see your content.

✦ Don't view a part of a video and then leave a comment or ask questions. Take the time to watch a full video before trying to engage.

✦ Do interact with people who leave comments. Read and respond to their remarks, and be gracious with a thank-you. Introduce them to your subscribers if you find their work valuable.

✦ Keep in mind that when you send a friend a YouTube video, negative or profane comments might be posted under it. Make sure children are not sent to YouTube videos if you know about disrespectful remarks posted at the bottom. Take the time to check out how the video displays. Even the most wholesome YouTube videos might have inappropriate viewer comments under them.

BLOGGING

A blog is like a person's private home in written form, where you are invited to see, smell, hear, and taste what they are all about. Just as etiquette applies when visiting private homes, it applies when visiting someone's virtual blog house. You venture into their blog and are exposed to the essence, culture, and ideas of the blogger.

There are many ways to become a community player and a friend in blog abodes, and many ways not to. Below are a few protocols to follow when entering, engaging, and becoming part of a person's blog.

- ✦ Be respectful of everyone's blog. It is an important aspect of blogging. A blog is someone's creation. You would never go into someone's house and stomp a vase or a piece of art they'd made. Instead, you might appreciate, make comments about, or have a healthy debate while admiring the art. Having a healthy debate doesn't mean you should say, "That vase is an ugly color!" It's much better to be subtle. Say something like "You sure chose an interesting color for that vase. I might have chosen green, not blue." It's a simple shift to use language that honors the creation.
- ✦ Again, as with visiting someone's house, when leaving a comment on someone's blog, be complimentary about your experience (reading the blog), pointing out the warmth, intellect, new ideas, or inspiration you encountered. To say something meaningful, you must commit to reading the entire post and also the title. You cannot comment on the essence and body of a home if you've only driven by, peeking quickly at the exterior. Putting your comments on another person's blog just so you will be seen and go viral

is called spammimg. Don't spam! It's the worst breach of etiquette in the blog world.

✦ Don't be too long and drawn out in your posts and other communications. Keep most of your blog short and to the point. Most readers don't have time to read blog posts that go on and on.

✦ Never steal another person's content. It's okay to admire, but never post it as your own. It is a nice gesture to feature another person's post on your blog; just get their permission, give them credit, and share a link back to their blog.

✦ It's polite to share if you've experienced something wonderful on someone's blog. You can share with your blog community and with virtual friends. Your virtual friends will be happy to be introduced to a new blog, and the blog owner will be grateful for the introduction.

✦ Keep your blog tidy, crisp, and clean with proper grammar, punctuation, and capitalization. Never use all caps; it's like shouting. Write in paragraphs; people's eyes glaze over if they have to read one long run-on sentence. Keep your written word clean—no inappropriate words or language.

✦ Keep in mind when you blog or comment on a blog that you aren't just inviting one person into your home, you are inviting all of cyberspace: every house, tent, castle, and hut in the world. So no posting questionable pictures of yourself. This goes for women *and* men. No pictures of you partying like it's 1999 or launching into a diatribe against your boss, company, or a political party. Keep a clean Web-print because future employers, bosses, in-laws, and prospective spouses will always be able to see and read it all. Think twice before pressing Post.

✦ If someone misbehaves on your blog house, don't comment back and don't engage. Simply delete what was said and don't waste a moment of your time with a disrespectful person. It's not your job to teach them good manners and etiquette. The faster you disengage, the faster they will be out of your blog and in search of someone else to take the bait. Refuse to play on their team by deleting what they say at the speed of light and saving your time for your positive blog participants.

+ Be gracious and considerate by thanking anyone who comments on your blog. You will want to comment back. If someone takes the time to remark on your blog, read what they've said and thank them for visiting. Also, if someone shares something heartfelt—a celebratory post, or a painful one about a tough time—on their blog, make a kind or encouraging comment. These go a long way to build trust and relationships. The virtual online community is exactly like those in the real world: we all want to be congratulated in times of celebration and acknowledged during difficult ones.

Four

TABLE MANNERS

It's Not Always About the Fork

I once interviewed a leading securities firm director about how she could gauge if a person was going to be a good fit with their firm. After an initial interview, if she was interested in the applicant, the follow-up interview would be over lunch. People disclose who they are when you break bread with them. From the minute they entered the restaurant, she observed how they interacted with the host. Did they pause to see where she would like them to sit? Did they let her lead the way to the table or did they lead? Did they pause before opening their menu or did they wait for her to open hers? The number-one thing she was eager to see was how they interacted with the waitstaff. Were they kind and considerate, or rude and abrupt? Did they order expensive items from the menu, or did they select a medium-price main course?

Social skills are extremely important. They are essential for personal and professional success, much more important than what fork to use, or where to place the napkin. Business attire, intelligence, and a solid education are all components to becoming a leader in business, but they don't mean anything without top-notch social skills as well. During the lunch, the director is also gauging how well the conversation flows. Is the candidate good at getting her to talk about her interests, where she went to school, her family, hobbies, and favorite vacation spots? And are they good at relaying their interests without disclosing anything too personal? This is important since we build true business relationships by opening up.

The most important thing to remember about table manners is to behave graciously. Everyone at the table should be enjoying both the meal and the company, not evaluating and judging each diner's familiarity with the rules of etiquette.

However, understanding a few basic rules will make you feel more comfortable at the table—whether you're at a dinner party, a work function, or with a friend at a nice restaurant. When you feel more comfortable, your companions will feel more comfortable, and the meal is likely to be a pleasant experience for everyone.

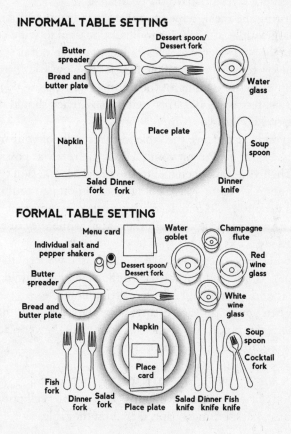

INFORMAL TABLE SETTING

Dessert spoon/ Dessert fork
Butter spreader
Bread and butter plate
Water glass
Napkin
Place plate
Soup spoon
Salad fork Dinner fork
Dinner knife

FORMAL TABLE SETTING

Menu card
Water goblet
Champagne flute
Individual salt and pepper shakers
Dessert spoon/ Dessert fork
Red wine glass
Butter spreader
Bread and butter plate
White wine glass
Napkin
Soup spoon
Place card
Cocktail fork
Fish fork
Place plate
Dinner fork Salad fork
Salad knife Dinner knife Fish knife

SITTING DOWN, USING NAPKINS, AND LEAVING THE TABLE

+ When you sit down at the table, place your purse behind you on your chair (if it's small enough) or on the floor at your feet. If you have a briefcase, put it on the floor next to your seat.

+ Sit up straight (remember that good posture demonstrates self-confidence) and keep your elbows off the table. Wait until your host picks up his napkin before placing your napkin on your lap. This should happen soon after sitting down, but not immediately upon being seated. If your host doesn't pick up his or her napkin, wait a minute or two, then place your napkin on your lap.

+ During the meal, remember that your napkin is not a washcloth or a tissue. It should not be used to wipe cutlery; just ask your server for clean silverware. Do not use your napkin to wash your whole face, or to blow your nose. If you need to do either of these things, just excuse yourself to the restroom. Napkins are not bibs. They should never be tucked into your shirt.

+ If you have to leave the table in the middle of your meal, place your napkin on your chair as discreetly as possible. When you leave the table to use the restroom, don't announce where you're going (e.g., "I gotta go to the bathroom"). No one needs the image of you in the restroom running through their head while they're eating. Just say, "Excuse me," and leave the table.

+ Sometimes when you leave the table, the waiter will fold your napkin and put it back on the table. Just unfold it and place it back on your lap after sitting down.

+ When you've finished eating, place the napkin on the table, semifolded, to the left of your plate. Never place the napkin in the middle of your plate.

GENERAL RULES FOR DINING

+ Don't place any personal items (such as your cell phone, purse, keys, business papers, etc.) on the table.

- Food is served from the left, and dishes are removed from the right.
- Wait for the host to take the first bite or for everyone to be served before you start eating. If more than six to eight people are at the table and hot food arrives, pause and look around the table. If no one says, "Go ahead and eat," you can ask your dining companions, "Shall we start?"
- Don't ask to taste someone else's food or offer anyone a taste of your food.
- Don't use your fingers to scoop food onto your fork.
- Don't talk with food in your mouth (your mother was right about this one!).
- Take small bites and keep your mouth closed while chewing.
- Never say anything negative about the food or bring attention to something you dislike. Everything you say should be gracious and positive.
- Pace yourself while eating so that you finish at approximately the same time as your host or the majority of diners.
- Never smoke at the table.
- Flatware is placed on the table in order of use, from the outside in, toward your plate. If two forks are on the table and you're not sure which to use first, use the one that is farthest from your plate.
- The salt and pepper travel together (like bride and groom). If someone asks for one of them, pass both together. The same rule applies to cream and sugar; they travel together.
- Once flatware is picked up, it should never touch the table again. Place flatware on the outer rim of your plate when you need to put it down, but make sure the handles aren't hanging off the plate like oars (they should be placed safely on the plate).

BREAD AND SOUP COURSES

Bread Course

The bread course is that, it's not the main course. The bread course is intended to be a light course before the soup, salad, and entrée arrive. Pace yourself and enjoy just one piece, maybe two. The bread plate causes so much confusion it's a wonder we use it. Be careful not to hijack your dining companion's bread plate: solids are placed on the left side, while liquids are on the right, and your bread plate should always be on your left.

Below are a few quick reminders about bread-course etiquette.

- Bread is passed to the right. A great way to remember this: if you passed to the left, you get *left* behind.
- The bread basket isn't passed hand to hand because it's awkward and it could get dropped. It should be placed on the table in front of the person, who will then serve himself.
- Don't "molest" the bread. You should only touch one piece, the one you've selected to take out of the basket.
- If the bread is in one large piece as opposed to individual rolls or slices and needs to be broken off, hold one side of the loaf with the napkin from the bread basket and tear off with your hand the piece you are taking. This will keep you from touching the bread in places that others will be eating.
- The butter dish will have a serving knife. Take a small serving of butter and place it on your bread plate. Be sure to return the butter server to the butter dish so others can serve themselves.
- Remember, your bread isn't cake, so don't frost the entire piece of bread nor saw the bread in half to receive the butter.
- Do tear off one bite-size piece of bread with your fingers and butter that one piece (on your plate, not in the air as if conducting an orchestra), then eat it. Never tear off more than one small piece at a time.

- When oil is on the table for everyone to use, don't dip your bread into it. Instead, spoon out a serving of oil and place it on your bread plate.
- Always rest your bread-and-butter knife on your bread plate, so the knife doesn't dirty the table or linens. The sharp side of the knife should face the center of the plate.

Soup Course

In general, foods are served from the left and liquids are served from the right. Soup is considered a food and should be served from the left.

The proper way to enjoy soup is to spoon it away from you and then bring the spoon up to your mouth (rather than hunkering down over the bowl). Then sip (don't slurp) from the side of the spoon. If you try to put the spoon straight into your mouth, your fellow diners will get an unexpected (and undesired) view of your tonsils.

Here are a few more tips for your soup course.

- Remember to keep your elbows close to your sides as you eat. You don't want to look like a buzzard about to take flight.
- If the soup is too hot, let it cool in the bowl. Never blow on it (you might end up spraying soup onto someone else). You can stir gently with your spoon to let cooler air move through the body of the bowl.
- For formal dining, it is not proper etiquette to dip bread in your soup.
- To get to that last bit of soup, tip your bowl away from you and spoon the soup in the same direction. *Do not* bring the entire bowl up to your face.
- When you're finished, rest your spoon on the saucer underneath the bowl. If there's no saucer, place the spoon in the soup bowl itself.

Bread Plate and Drinks

Which drink is yours? Often this is one of the first questions asked when dining out. Your bread plate will be to your left, and your drink will be to your right.

Here are a few easy tips that will help you remember.

+ Hold your hands in front of you with your palms facing in. Make the universal okay sign with both hands. Looking down at your hands, you should see that your left hand has formed a *b* (*b*read plate) and your right hand has formed a *d* (*d*rink).
+ You could also think of the acronym BMW, which stands for "bread, meal, water" (the order in which those items are placed, from left to right).

- When taking a drink, try to look down into your glass. It looks funny when you're drinking and looking around at the same time. If your glass has a stem, hold it by the stem. If you need to practice this at home to make sure you don't spill, go ahead and practice! It's better to spill at home than at a formal dinner.
- Don't eat the fruit out of a drink until the entire drink has been consumed.
- If your neighbor has hijacked your bread plate, use the left side of your dinner plate to hold your bread.
- If someone accidentally drinks from your glass, without causing a commotion discreetly ask your waiter for another one.

ENTRÉES: CONTINENTAL / AMERICAN

There are two styles of main-course cutting: Continental and American. No matter which style you use, the following rules apply.

- Hold the knife in your dominant hand (so if you're right-handed, hold the knife in your right hand) and the fork in your other hand.
- Cut one piece of meat at a time, and don't "saw" it by dragging the knife back and forth (there's no need to reslaughter the meat). Instead, place the knife at the top and then pull it back toward your rib cage. Repeat as necessary.

After this stage, the two styles diverge.

- With the American style, after you have cut each piece of meat, you lay the knife down at the top of your plate with the blade facing toward you, put the fork in your dominant hand, and bring the fork to your mouth with the tines facing up.

AMERICAN- AND CONTINENTAL-STYLE CUTTING

- ■ HOLD KNIFE IN DOMINANT HAND
- ■ HOLD FORK WITH TINES FACING DOWN
- ■ CUT ONE PIECE OF MEAT AT A TIME
- ■ DON'T "SAW" THE MEAT. PULL THE KNIFE TOWARD YOUR RIB CAGE AND REPEAT AS NECESSARY

- ■ HOLD FORK IN NONDOMINANT HAND
- ■ KEEP KNIFE IN HAND WHILE EATING
- ■ FORK TINES FACING DOWN

CONTINENTAL-STYLE EATING

RESTING   FINISHED
- ■ FORK TINES FACING DOWN

- ■ LAY KNIFE ON PLATE
- ■ SWITCH FORK TO DOMINANT HAND
- ■ FORK TINES FACING UP

AMERICAN-STYLE EATING

RESTING   FINISHED
- ■ FORK TINES FACING UP

◆ In the Continental style, instead of putting the knife down and switching the fork to your dominant hand after each cut, keep the fork in your nondominant hand and bring it up to your mouth with the tines facing down. Since you're keeping the knife in your hand throughout most of the meal, it's important not to use that hand to gesture as you're talking.

◆ Choose which style of main-course cutting you are most comfortable with.

◆ However, if everyone at your table is using the same style, you might want to join them. Consider practicing both styles at home so that you are comfortable either way and can easily adapt to any situation.

+ During the meal, if you need to put your fork and knife down but you are not yet finished eating, place the knife and fork in the "resting" position, as illustrated (opposite). When you're finished, the knife and fork should be placed diagonally on your plate, with the tops/tips in the "ten o'clock" position and the bottoms/handles in the "four o'clock" position with knife blade facing inward toward you.

DINNER PARTIES: HOST AND GUEST RESPONSIBILITIES

If you are hosting a dinner party or going to someone else's home as a guest, you will want your part in the event to be a success. Whether host or guest, following the guidelines below will ensure success.

HOST DUTIES

+ The number-one rule of hosting a dinner party is "the guests come first." Plain and simple, they get the finest seats in the house, are served premium fare, and enjoy both choice of everything and an impressive portion of dessert.

+ Welcome guests as soon as they arrive. After you show them where to put their coats, purses, etc., introduce them to at least one other person, preferably someone you feel they will connect with.

+ The host sets the mood, so no flailing around like an exasperated chicken with its head cut off. Keep the food, drinks, and plans simple. The focus should be on the people, not the flaming soufflé.

+ Be a diplomat and steer conversations that aren't appropriate to clearer waters. When you see a guest in the clutches of Long-Winded Larry, save them by motioning for him to help you in the kitchen. Seat people who know each other together, and place talkative people in the middle of the table on the long sides, so they can help keep the conversation going.

+ There is a big difference between etiquette and manners. Etiquette dictates that you should never eat your salad with your main-course fork. Manners dictate that you would never mention the mistake. Kindness is the number-one rule of manners, so make sure that's your number-one goal when hosting or attending a dinner party.

GUEST DUTIES

+ As soon as you get an invitation, look at your calendar and RSVP. The first thing out of your mouth when you call the host to respond should always be "Thank you so much for the invitation." This rule has no exceptions, whether you are able to attend or not.

+ Ask if you can bring anything and suggest items that you can provide, such as a salad or dessert. Offer something that you are proficient at making and that is appropriate for the occasion.

+ Mark the party date on your calendar and save the invitation to remind you of the time, address, and dress code.

+ If you are close friends or a family member, call the day before or the day of the dinner party and ask if you can do anything to help, or if you can pick anything up on your way. If they need something, you will be a lifesaver.

+ Always take a host gift. Make sure it is something the host doesn't have to stop what they are doing to tend to, such as flowers without a vase. If you bring wine, tell the host that it's to enjoy at a later date, as they usually already have the wine paired with the dinner. Some great host gift ideas are unscented candles, CDs, a book, or coasters.

- When you arrive, offer to help with any preparations that still need tending. Look around. If veggies need to be sliced, ask if you could help slice them.
- Your job as a guest is to mingle, mingle, mingle! Do your part to help make the party a success by talking about topical interests, steering clear of negative news or things that are too personal. If you see a guest who seems shy, engage them in conversation by asking such questions as "How do you know [the host]?" You can talk about current events, holiday plans, vacations, hobbies, etc.
- After the dinner, once again jump in and help with the cleanup. You don't need to ask for permission since you know the help will be more than appreciated. However, if you are asked not to help, don't press it.
- When it's time to leave, be sure to thank the hosts for the time they spent preparing for the party and opening up their home to you. Everyone likes to feel appreciated. Compliment them on the wonderful company and great food. Even if you don't ask for the turtle soup recipe, you can always find something to rave about. Remember to send a thank-you note the next day.

BANQUETS AND BUFFETS

Even though buffets are informal, they still work best when attendees practice decorum.

Buffets are a wonderful way to provide many different food options, but I must caution you that eating a buffet into bankruptcy may derail your chances of corporate advancement.

Here are a few tips for protocol at a buffet.

- Be an Eagle Scout and do a walk-through of the entire buffet before you start to serve yourself. Scope out your top three choices and start there. Save the second trip to the buffet for things that are of interest, different from what you usually eat, etc.

- Plate etiquette: Always get a clean plate for each trip you make to the buffet. Remember, it's not a platter, it's a plate. Only put two servings, maybe three, onto your plate at one time, keeping in mind you can go back again and again. Always place your napkin in your chair when making a return trip to the buffet line.
- Be patient, not pushy. Walk with the people going to the buffet line, not through them. You aren't in a speed-walking competition. Be patient and wait to serve yourself once the line moves along. Be mindful not to reach through or in front of people.
- No snacking in the buffet line. Eating in the buffet line is not sanitary and will dull your appetite. Furthermore, it slows the line down for you and others. Remember, the buffet line is not intended to be a food-sampling extravaganza.
- Return serving utensils to their original dishes, to keep flavors and foods from cross-pollinating. Never serve yourself from the same serving dish from which someone else is serving themselves, even if more than one serving spoon is provided.
- Dessert tips: I say eat dessert first, but I don't advise doing this in front of your children. Serve yourself dessert by the same rules as the main course: only place two or three servings on your plate at one time and remember you can go up again.
- Do you tip at a buffet? Yes! The waitstaff are refilling your drink glasses, removing plates, and helping to keep your table nice and neat. Tip 15 to 20 percent of your bill. Keep in mind the staff services your table more times than at a traditional order-off-the-menu restaurant.

TABOO TABLE TOPICS

- You should never discuss a few "taboo" topics while dining: surgery, divorce, finances, religion, and any other topic that's too personal or too negative. The dinner table is not a good place to push political views on others, or to complain endlessly about your boss.

✦ If someone is led to say "too much information," you can bet the topic isn't dining conversation. Avoid bathroom humor and gross subjects. If in doubt, it is always better to share less information than more.

✦ Focus on the people you are dining with and offer up a genuine compliment. Make it something that will lead to further conversation. You can inquire about family, the latest hot spots to eat or hang out, movies, books, music, etc.

✦ Meals should be pleasant affairs, so try to keep the conversation positive and upbeat. Talk about your recent travels, new hobbies, extracurricular activities, and other exciting things going on in your life. Read the newspaper or scan the Internet for news before going out so that you can speak intelligently about current events.

✦ If you make interesting, useful, and positive contributions to the conversation, you are more likely to be invited to the next social event.

WINE ETIQUETTE

Mark Twain once said, "There are no standards of taste in wine, cigars, poetry, prose, etc. Each man's own taste is the standard, and a majority vote cannot decide for him, or in any slightest degree affect the supremacy of his own standard."

When choosing wine, the old standard of reds with red meat and whites with chicken and fish is no longer the guideline. The main thing to remember is to choose a wine that doesn't overpower the food you are serving. You want the wine to compliment the foods and desserts.

Here are a few guidelines.

WHITE WINES

+ Full-bodied: oak accent, rich aroma—goes well with creamy seafood, chicken, pork, and spicy dishes. Examples: oaked chardonnay, Rhine
+ Medium-bodied: smooth, fruity, and mild—goes well with hearty seafood and chicken. Examples: chardonnay, sauvignon blanc
+ Light-bodied: slightly sweet and fruity—goes well with salads, vegetables, and light seafood. Examples: Chablis, sauterne, chenin blanc

RED WINES

+ Full-bodied: bold, intense flavor, dry—goes well with braised dishes, red meats, and vintage cheeses. Examples: Chianti, cabernet sauvignon, Bordeaux
+ Medium-bodied: smooth, slightly fruity, and mild—goes well with chicken, beef, and pizza. Examples: burgundy, pinot noir, merlot
+ Light-bodied: fruity and floral—goes well with light fish, chicken, pasta, sandwiches, and light appetizers. Examples: zinfandel, Beaujolais

When preparing for a cocktail party, think 55 percent white and 45 percent red. Always have more on hand than you think you will need. Each bottle has five servings, so for a three-to-four-hour party with eight wine drinkers, you will need twenty-four servings, or about three servings per person, so six or seven bottles should suffice.

When sampling wine, the waiter will present the bottle for you to view. Don't touch the bottle since you are only looking to see that it's the wine you ordered. View the label, and if it is indeed the one you ordered, just nod. The cork will then be presented to you. Don't sniff it; just glance at or squeeze it to make sure it isn't dried out. There is no need to smell the cork, as you will taste a small serving next and have the opportunity then to smell it. Taste the small sample poured for you and again nod if it's to your liking. No need to go into a diatribe, just nod with approval, so your guests can be served. If by some rare chance the wine isn't to your liking and you have to send it back, do so simply without a big reaction.

Below are a few dos and don'ts to keep in mind that will enhance your wine awareness and experience.

- ✦ Don't store wine in a vertical position as the cork will dry out.
- ✦ Don't store wines in hot places such as on the top of your refrigerator or in the trunk of a vehicle.
- ✦ Do ask the waiter or server if you don't understand certain terminology.
- ✦ Do ignore wine snobs. A real wine lover wants to teach, share, and educate, not intimidate.
- ✦ Don't fill a glass more than half-full.
- ✦ Do let red wine breathe for forty-five minutes to an hour before drinking it.
- ✦ Don't become exasperated if wine is spilled; just use sparkling water to blot the area.
- ✦ Do have nonalcoholic drinks on hand for nondrinkers.
- ✦ Do store wines bottles that aren't finished in the refrigerator.
- ✦ Do accept that good wines can come in bottles with screw-on tops.

TOASTS

The host should always be the first to offer a toast. If you're giving a toast, remember to prepare your words ahead of time. Stand up, keep it short, and make it clear when you've finished. Ending with a simple "Cheers!" will do the trick.

Here's a good example: "I'd like to toast our guest of honor this evening, Mr. Charles Philips. Mr. Philips is both an extremely successful entrepreneur and a generous philanthropist, and I am honored that he has chosen to spend this evening with us. Mr. Philips, on behalf of all of us, thank you for being here. It is a pleasure to have you with us tonight. Cheers!"

When you're being toasted, don't touch or even look at your glass (that would be like cheering for yourself). You should return the toast, however. Simply stand up when the toast is finished and say something like "Thank you so much for inviting me here tonight. I want you to know that the feeling is mutual. I am honored to be here and feel privileged to be in such wonderful company. Here's to a wonderful evening!" Whatever you say, try to keep it to less than thirty seconds and sixty at most. Then you can take a sip of your drink!

Here are a few more toasting tips.

+ When giving a toast, always stand up, be sincere, and keep it short and simple.

- If the group is large, it is not mandatory to clink glasses when a toast is made. Just raise your glass and take a sip, but do not guzzle.
- In a small group, always look the other people in the eyes when you (gently) clink their glass and say "Cheers."
- Although traditional, alcohol is not necessary to perform a toast. Sparkling fruit juice, punch, or even soda may be used.
- When toasting someone, be yourself and talk as you normally would. Try to look around the room at everyone and speak loudly enough for everyone to hear.
- If you are nervous about giving a toast, practice it over and over until you feel more confident. Then try practicing in front of one or two friends.
- Jokes can be great, but don't tell inside jokes. You want to make sure everyone listening to you is able to understand.
- Always keep what you say appropriate and make sure to stay sober. Remember, it's not about you, and keep in mind your toast may be on video for many years to come.
- If you know you just won't feel comfortable giving a toast, then it is okay to decline. Just explain (ahead of time) that you are not ready to do it.

Five

BUSINESS MATTERS

Sometimes Talent Isn't Enough

Once I spent an afternoon in the office of a New York entertainment agency. They asked me to listen to two artists who had submitted demos of their pop songs. After I listened to both, I thought that one was clearly more talented than the other. One was more polished and clear in his vocals and melody, while the other was raw vocally and the song wasn't mixed well. I also looked at their press kits and headshots and tried to see how they related to mainstream music. The headshots showed warmth and clarity across the board.

The next step was sitting in on their personal interviews to see how they related socially, as these were two artists who would be singing mainstream pop music, not heavy metal or grunge, where manners and public image were not as essential.

I initially liked the more talented artist, of course. Most of you would have agreed. The interview started in the limo, where the more talented artist put up the window as soon as he climbed in. He didn't engage the limo driver. He barely made eye contact while getting out and saying thank you. He neglected to hold the door for the man walking close behind him with his hands full of coffee cups. He arrived at the agency office and barely spoke to the receptionist. He just blurted out, "I'm here to see Mr. Big Executive." There was no smile, no "Good morning," no "How are you?" He just sat down and talked loudly on his cell phone to one of his friends. After another fifteen minutes of meeting with him, we were less than impressed.

We took a break and came back for the second interview. The artist jumped in the limo and rode with his arms propped up on the divider. He talked to the limo driver the entire way about where he was going and how excited and nervous he was. He thanked the driver, saying, "So long, Pops," and headed into the building. He held the elevator for a young mom pushing a stroller and spoke to her the entire ride to the twentieth floor. Next, he walked into the office and said, "Hello, how are you?" and waited for a response from the receptionist. He then introduced himself and said he had an appointment with Mr. Big Executive at twelve-thirty.

A few weeks later I learned that the second artist was given the recording contract, and the agency also signed him for live-appearance bookings. When I asked why, the head of the agency said he was a good singer, much better than his demo, which was recorded from home on inferior equipment. He said any good producer could improve the recording flaws in the studio. The clincher was how he shone across all situations. He would naturally be more marketable to the ticket- and album-buying public, as well as in the social media. If someone starts out with great people skills, they have an edge everywhere, and people skills come from conscious behavior and good manners.

BUSINESS CARDS

Exchanging business cards offers the perfect opportunity to build a new relationship by showing interest and respect. It's a quick social exchange, but holds a lot of weight if done properly.

When a business card is offered, it is important to pause, look, and take the time to demonstrate interest in the person who gave it. This shows you value the person, her card, and also her company. Don't slip the card in your pocket without a glance while yammering on.

Below are a few more tips about business cards.

- Business cards are an extension of you. Avoid handing them out in a wanton manner as if you were in Times Square handing out flyers!
- Your business card is like your résumé. Keep it crisp, clean, and current. No marked-out numbers or e-mails. It is a physical extension of you, so let it represent you in the best way possible.
- Ask permission before giving someone your business card. Simply say, "May I give you my card?"
- Be confident and composed when giving out your business card.
- You want to appear prepared and at ease when taking out your business card, not as if your clothes are ablaze and you're trying to put out a fire.

- Present your business card with your right hand or both hands with your logo facing the recipient so your name, logo, company, and title can easily be read.
- Never give your business card with your left hand, as it is considered rude and disrespectful in several cultures globally.
- Take a business card with your right hand or with both hands. Be sure to say "Thank you" while taking a moment to glance at the card and remark about the logo, colors, company, etc. Use this brief opportunity to find out something about the person, even if it's simply how long they've worked at company X.
- Be careful not to jot notes on another person's card.
- Never put a person's business card in your back pocket or wallet and sit on it. It's like plopping down on someone's head. Respect dictates that you put another person's card in your suit-jacket pocket and never in a pocket below the belt. You can put the card into a nice cardholder, sending a nonverbal show of respect and safekeeping.
- If you are wearing a suit jacket, you can have a pocket for outgoing cards and a pocket for incoming cards. If you aren't wearing a suit jacket, keeping your personal cards and newly received cards in a clutch or business-card holder is another savvy solution.
- Never, ever leave home without your business cards or say "I forgot them." You will come across as absentminded and unprofessional.

BUSINESS LUNCHES: HOST AND GUEST RESPONSIBILITIES

Breaking bread is the oldest and best way to build relationships, establish trust, and enhance the growth of your company.

Here are a few protocols for the host, as well as the guest, to follow to ensure a successful business lunch.

HOST DUTIES

+ Inviting your guest to lunch is the first step. Simply say, "I would like you to be my guest for lunch."

+ You choose the restaurant, making sure it has options for vegetarians as well as carnivores. Be certain it's a restaurant you are comfortable with, so that you know the best table to do business at with the fewest interruptions. Don't choose a table by the kitchen or busy walkways. Ask for the most professional waiter, one you are familiar with.

+ Arrive fifteen minutes early to look over your table, the menu, and to speak to the waiter about how you prefer things to go. Take a second to talk to your waiter to catch up and give any special instructions before your guest arrives. Let the waiter know if you want bread and water on the table right away, or if they should be brought once you and your guest have started talking.

+ You have three choices of where to meet and greet your guest—the bar, the lobby, or your table. If it is a nicer restaurant and your guest can be escorted to the table, then that is the best place to receive your client. When guests approach, stand up and greet them. The second-best place to meet is in the lobby, so you can walk to the table together. The bar isn't the best choice for meeting.

+ The guest gets the seat of honor facing the restaurant, waterfall, artwork, or golf course. Be careful not to block or box the guest in with a view of the corner or bathrooms.

+ A lunch meeting is a time to get to know your client and build relationships. Talk about points of interest—where the client went to college, favorite sports teams, recent vacation locations, hobbies, family, etc. Don't launch right into business: establish some commonality, trust, and familiarity first. The best time to talk about business is during dessert and/or coffee, unless clients indicate they are ready to discuss business sooner.

+ Let your guests know that they have any option on the menu, offering a drink, appetizers, etc., mentioning, for example, that the stuffed-mushroom appetizers are great and the restaurant is known for its sea bass entrée.

+ Make sure nothing is on the table—no papers, cell phones, keys, etc. They are distractions. Never, ever talk on your cell phone or text during a lunch meeting. All attention should be on the client. If you must go to the bathroom, say, "Excuse me for a moment," and place your napkin on your chair. There is no need to announce where you are going.

+ The most graceful way to pay is for the bill never to reach the table. When you arrive early, give your credit card to the waiter, hostess, or maître d' and say you will take care of the bill when the client has left the building.

+ Walk your clients to the lobby or to their car at the end of the meeting and thank them for having lunch with you.

GUEST DUTIES

+ Arrive on time. This will show that you are punctual and grateful for the invitation. If you get held up in traffic or a meeting, always call the restaurant or your hosts to let them know you might be a few minutes late.

+ Don't order messy foods, such as ribs, spaghetti, or crab legs. You are there to build your business relationship, so the focus isn't on eating. Order something easy to eat that isn't the most expensive item on the menu.

+ Be a gracious guest. Share your points of interest—that you enjoy archery, hiking, or fly-fishing, that you are an avid art lover and enjoy photojournaling. Also, contribute a little about where you attended college, your favorite hockey team or Broadway play. Never, ever share anything too personal. Keep the conversation upbeat and entertaining. Make sure you learn about your host's interests and life as well. Never talk or text on your phone while at a lunch meeting. This shows disrespect and takes the focus and significance off the host.

- Compliment the choice of restaurant and thank your host for a wonderful meal. Send a thank-you note, mentioning something that holds value with your host or something your host shared with you during the lunch meeting—for example: "Enjoy your upcoming hiking trip."

CASUAL FRIDAY

It's a nice change of pace to be able to dress down one day a week when you go to work, but casual Fridays are still workdays. Keep in mind it's all about being *le chic,* and not *le freak.* Examples: *le chic*—crisp, clean, and conservative. *Le freak*—hair jacked to heaven, shoes so high and chunky you're about to blow an ankle, or Crocs; worse yet, Crocs with socks.

Here are a few more tips to keep in mind when picking out our clothes for work on Casual Friday.

- Avoid wearing anything that you might wear to the beach, baseball game, or backyard barbecue. This means no flip-flops, belly tops, miniskirts, belly shirts, baggy pants, skintight jeans, or anything that allows others to see your Underoos. All of the above are strictly forbidden.
- Ripped and holey are what one hopes to see at the gym and at worship services, not in your clothing at work.
- Sweatpants, sweatshirts, and other forms of workout clothes are taking the word *casual* a bit too far, even if they are glittery or have fancy words written across them. Also avoid pajama pants, since they shouldn't even be worn down your driveway to get the mail.
- In clothing and jewelry, simplicity makes an elegant statement. So no clanking, dangly bracelets or necklaces. You don't want to look like a walking yard sale. And men, when it comes to jewelry, less is better. Think Clooney, not Mr. T.
- It's a competitive society, so anything we can do to set ourselves apart from other people is always a plus. When in

doubt, ask yourself, "If I ran into my minister, CEO, or Aunt Gertie, would I feel polished, professional, and proud?"

✦ If you are still uncertain about what's acceptable, ask a supervisor. It's better to find out in advance than be corrected later.

CONFERENCING: BUSINESS MEETINGS / TELECONFERENCES / VIDEOCONFERENCES

If you want to succeed in business, it's important to make a good impression in the eyes of your colleagues, bosses, and clients. How you conduct yourself in a meeting will suggest your level of professionalism and how well you perform on your job.

Here are some tips for your next business meeting or conference.

BUSINESS MEETINGS

✦ Make sure you are appropriately dressed. If you don't know what to wear, it's always best to dress up rather than down and be conservative.

✦ It's important to be on time or even a little early, and make sure you have allotted enough time to conduct all business necessary. You do not want to rush things along just because you have somewhere else to go before the meeting has naturally ended.

✦ Turn off your cell phone before entering the meeting: your focus should be 100 percent on the business at hand and the people in attendance.

✦ When you arrive, look around the room and acknowledge each attendee. Say hello to the people you know by name, and write down the names of anyone you've just been introduced to.

✦ Come prepared to contribute to the meeting by participating in discussions, taking notes, and sharing information.

✦ If taking notes on your laptop, engage with other people in the meeting before logging on. Never surf the Web during a meeting or go on your social media sites.

- Always use good manners: *please* and *thank you* never go out of style. Maintain a positive attitude and never speak negatively about others. If you disagree with someone's view, acknowledge them and state that you would like to add another option or idea.
- Don't interrupt anyone who is speaking, but be prepared to speak up when the time is right. Make sure you stay on topic and always respect the viewpoints of others.
- Don't be a distraction by getting up and down to get something to drink or to go to the restroom. This is seen as attention seeking. If refreshments are available in the room, serve yourself before the meeting starts. In this case it is fine to eat during the meeting and also enjoy the drinks and coffee provided. Resist the urge to linger over the refreshments.
- What is shared in the meeting should be considered confidential, unless otherwise stated, and not shared with anyone who was not in attendance.

TELECONFERENCES

- Before the teleconference begins, make sure all participants will be available at the same time and that they have the necessary technology available for it.
- E-mail the agenda in advance of the conference so as not to waste any time while on the phone, and be sure to include your company guidelines and teleconference etiquette so each participant is well prepared.
- Make sure there isn't any background noise that will make it difficult to hear one another.
- Once your phone conference begins, introduce all attendees. Everyone should say hello and their name so you hear each person's voice. If someone joins in after the conference has begun, be sure to introduce that person as well.
- Be sure to state your name before questions or input: "It's Harrison with a question about the Gatti contract."

- Because participants cannot see each other, it is important to pause to allow people to interject and ask questions. Since you cannot see each other's nonverbal cues, you will have to ask your listeners if they understand what you are trying to convey.
- When the conference is over, allow each person to provide feedback; e-mail works well for this purpose. You can ask if the participants felt the meeting went well and if the teleconference technology was effective.

VIDEOCONFERENCES

- Before the meeting, prepare an agenda and send it to all participants, not just those in the room with you.
- Be sure to dress in clothes that are easy on the eyes, nothing flashy that may cause a glare, including clunky, clanging jewelry.
- Eliminate background noise and anything else that could possibly be a distraction.
- Arrive early to test your equipment and make sure everyone is in their seats, then arrange your camera so each person is clearly visible and place the microphone where everyone can be heard.
- Choose one person from each location to ask and answer questions so you won't have everyone talking at the same time.
- Be sure to introduce everyone and possibly wear name tags if people don't know each other.
- People should just be themselves, speaking and gesturing as they normally would, looking straight into the camera. Given the one-second audio delay, speak clearly and leave time at the end of each statement for complete audio transmission.
- Make sure you are focused on the meeting at hand and not checking text messages or trying to get other work done while conferencing. Give the attendees your undivided attention.

- If you are speaking, don't move and gesture too much, as this may distort the picture and cause a delay in communication.
- Keep your hands away from your face and refrain from touching your hair.

HOME OFFICE

If you are self-employed or work at home for a corporation, following is a work-at-home protocol that will ensure personal and corporate success.

SET YOUR AGENDA OR SCHEDULE AND FOLLOW IT. E-MAIL, TEXTING, AND SOCIAL NETWORKING ARE IMPORTANT, BUT MUST BE USED IN A LIMITED FASHION. SET AND FOLLOW TIME PARAMETERS.

ESTABLISH BOUNDARIES WITH YOUR FRIENDS, CHILDREN, SPOUSE, AND NEIGHBORS. LET THEM KNOW YOU KEEP A TIGHT OFFICE SCHEDULE.

KEEP YOUR PERSONAL COMMENTS OUT OF BUSINESS CONVERSATIONS. MAINTAIN YOUR PROFESSIONAL PERSONA.

OPEN AND CLOSE SHOP AT THE SAME TIME EVERY DAY. TREAT YOUR BUSINESS LIKE A BUSINESS AND OTHERS WILL AS WELL.

- Set your agenda or schedule and follow it.
- Dress the part. If you wouldn't do business in your husband's boxers or your wife's robe, then don't wear them when you start your business day.
- Avoid snack attacks. Taking little bites here and there adds up—the freshman fifteen doesn't look good or sit well on any of us.
- Beware of time-wasting activities that are dressed up like business opportunities. E-mail, texting, Skype, Twitter, Facebook, and LinkedIn are all important but must be utilized in a limited fashion. Set time parameters and stick to them.
- Keep your professional persona. Don't relax your boundaries just because you're at home. You're in your home *office,* so comments of a personal nature should be kept out of business conversations. People don't want to know you haven't brushed, had a fuss with your spouse, or haven't changed your clothes in two days.
- Set boundaries with your friends, children, spouse, and neighbors. They need to know you keep a tight office schedule and that they can't just stop by and plunk down for a twenty-minute coffee klatch.
- Do not allow background noise from your children, pets, radio, or television when you are on a business call.
- Avoid using your home address for business. A post office box will appear more professional and will offer security, privacy, and separation of "church and state."
- Open and close shop at the same time every single business day. Fifteen minutes before closing time, read over your list of things to accomplish. Check off things completed and start a list of things to tackle the next day.
- Treat your business as a business and others will treat it like a business as well.

INTERVIEW NECESSITIES

When preparing for an interview, be sure to research the company first. Look for them on Google and any social media networks you find them linked to. If they are on Facebook, Twitter, and LinkedIn, read their latest posts. Also, try to find out a little about the person who will be interviewing you. Know the company's mission statement and study their Web site. If you know anyone who works for them, ask for details about the company. Know if they are a national, international, or regional company and if the company has been in the news lately.

Here are a few more tips before going on that important interview.

+ Be on time. What is considered on time? In this context, ten minutes early. Arriving ten minutes early will let you get settled and mentally prepared. It will give you a few minutes to go over things you need to remember about the company and to review the questions you want to ask. Although fewer people are wearing watches today, as they rely on cell phones for time management, a watch is a nice accessory to wear on an interview. It visually conveys that you are time-conscious.
+ The interview starts the moment you get out of your car. Be sure to speak to everyone you come into contact with—the parking attendant, people in the elevator, and especially the receptionist. They are a direct link to the person who is interviewing you, so treat each and every person with respect.
+ Turn off your smartphone, iPod, and iPad. In fact, leave them in the car. You don't want your phone to ring, buzz, or vibrate during the interview. Also, glancing down to look at text messages is almost an involuntary response these days, practically like breathing, so keep temptation out of the way.
+ You want your clothing to mimic the style, tone, and dress

that the company follows. When in doubt, kick it up a few notches. It's better to be overdressed than underdressed. Never wear perfume and keep accessories to a minimum.

✦ Your shoes tell a story. Let the story be shiny and well kept, without scratches or wear and tear on the heels.

✦ The best things to bring: a warm smile, confident eye contact, good posture, and a snug, committed web-to-web handshake.

✦ Meet and greet. The first seven seconds you meet someone are the most vital. Know how to give the best handshake. The six different handshakes all convey different meanings, but there is only one right way. A handshake is the only physical contact you are going to have with that individual, so make it work for you. Make sure you smile and make confident eye contact. Always shake hands while standing, never while in a seated or subservient position.

✦ Wow them with your graciousness. A thank-you note received within twenty-four hours of the interview is like liquid gold. It hits many senses. It's tactile: people touch it. It's visual: they read it. It gives the interviewer another opportunity to think about you. It's one more way to be seen in a positive light. Write it in your car after the interview. Drive to the nearest post office and mail it immediately. The sooner you write and mail your thank-you note, the less you have to labor over it.

NETWORKING–BUILDING NEW AND LASTING RELATIONSHIPS

When going to a networking event, arrive early and don't linger to the very end. Know going in the most important people you want to connect with and get to them early, while they and you are fresh, energetic, and on top of their game. You must take nine magical steps to ensure a successful and worthwhile event. I'll break them down into three sets of three.

THE FIRST THREE PREP STEPS

✦ Know who and what the organization is about. Try your
best to read about the people attending so you will know
a little about them going in. With so much posted on
Facebook, Twitter, Google, and LinkedIn, it should be
easy to get solid information and possibly pictures of
previous networking events so you can see the tone and
formality of the event and the level of dress and follow
suit.

✦ Be certain you have a solid, interesting, and crisp personal
introduction ready. Instead of saying, "I'm a financial
planner," you could say, "I help people live comfortable
and affluent lives by teaching them a few basic steps to take
and dangers to avoid."

✦ Don't forget your business cards. Have them in an easy-to-
access case or pocket.

THE NEXT THREE PREP STEPS

✦ Go with the intention of speaking with the event organizer, registration or sign-in person, and also the speaker.

✦ Thank them for putting the event together and also ask
how you can be of help.

✦ Ask the organizers if they would like you to speak with
anyone in particular. In return, ask them who they think
the three best people are for *you* to meet.

THE LAST THREE STEPS

✦ Make sure you aren't the last person lingering, unless you
are the event organizer. Appear as though you've got
things to do and are on the ball. You've added value to
other people's businesses and gained new business
relationships. It's time to make an exit.

✦ Before leaving, find the people who headed the event and
thank them. Then find the people you made a great
connection with and tell them good-bye and how nice it
was to meet them.

✦ Write a handwritten note to the speaker, the event head, and the person who did the registering. They know all the people at the event and many of the ones you weren't able to talk to or connect with. You want them to remember you, and writing a thank-you note puts you head and shoulders above everyone else. When the group is looking for a person in your field of expertise, they might suggest you because you took the time to talk to them, thank them in person, and follow up with a note.

Below are a few tips on how to shine like a new dime while at the event.

✦ **Best in show.** The best spot in the room is closest to the door, so you can speak to the people that you want to talk to and catch them early while they are alert, fresh, and not talked out.

✦ **The worst spot in the room is by the bar or buffet.** You aren't there to eat. You are there to build business relationships, so eat before you go. It would also be a wise choice to forgo the alcoholic beverages (the bartender doesn't count as a new business relationship) so you are together, alert, and professional. Always face the entrance no matter where you are in the room, never have your back facing the door.

✦ **How to become part of a group.** Approach people standing alone or in groups of three or more. Move toward the group, smile, and make eye contact with one or two of the people and wait for a lull in the conversation, then jump in with a word or two. Never interrupt two people who are intensely conversing.

✦ **Resist the ol' chain gang.** Don't hang out with the people you already know. It might be comfortable and not require a lot of work, but you have to remember why you are there: to build *new* relationships. It's fine to check in with acquaintances and strengthen your established relationships; just don't hang out with them the entire evening.

+ **Escaping the conversational rambler.** Listen for a respectable three to four minutes, then say, "It was great talking with you. Now, I must go say hello and thank the host," or, "I see a colleague I must connect with again, great to meet you, have a nice evening."

+ **Remember business-card protocol.** When you have the opportunity to give or accept a business card, it's a wonderful way to show respect, build rapport, and learn more about a person. Have a set place for incoming and outgoing cards, so you aren't doing break-dance moves trying to make the exchange. You want it to be smooth and respectful, not flustered and haphazard. Don't just shove the card in a pocket, take a second to look at it and comment. Your business card is an extension of you. Make sure it is in the best shape possible: clean and without creases, writing, or smudge marks.

OFFICE CUBICLES

Cubicles are where we daily drop anchor to do our job. While it is our haven to create, soar, hide, and sometimes even sleep, remember that other people are affected by our daily rituals and routines even when we're hidden away in a cubicle.

Here are a few guidelines for visiting or inhabiting a cubicle.

+ No bursting into someone's cubicle. Just because it doesn't have a door doesn't mean you have an All-Access Pass to barge in and move about the cabin.
+ Knock lightly on the wall, make eye contact, and announce yourself in the doorway before entering.
+ If someone's on the phone, don't loom around the cubicle waiting for them to finish. Simply come back later.
+ Attempt to answer your phone on the first or second ring and keep the ringer volume low. Limit the use of

speakerphones, and use meeting rooms for conference calls whenever possible.

+ When talking on the phone, remember to use your library voice. With personal or sensitive calls, remember that your coworkers can hear your end of the conversation.

+ Don't yell across cubes. Get up and go to your coworker's cube to conduct business or use e-mail or instant messaging.

+ When you are busy at work and you don't want to be interrupted, try saying, "I'm swamped. If you need me, can you catch me later?" If that doesn't work, you can hang a sign in your doorway that says DO NOT DISTURB.

+ A cubicle isn't an open-air flea market, so don't hover over the top or paw people's staplers, paper clips, or personal items.

+ Don't read someone's computer screen or comment on a conversation you overheard, and resist answering a question that was directed to someone in the cube next to yours.

+ Never, ever heat or eat hot food in your cubicle. Not only does that garlic chicken stink up the joint, it may linger for days.
+ Avoid popping gum, slurping drinks, humming, and tapping or clicking pens.
+ Please keep your shoes on. No matter how much your coworkers love you, they don't want to smell your feet or see your bunions.

OFFICE PARTIES

Mingle, mingle, and mingle some more. Arrive on time; don't hang out with the same old office friends in a clique all night. Step out of your comfort zone. Introduce yourself to everyone and have a few icebreakers ready such as "What are your travel plans for the holidays?" Never be the last to leave. Nothing is worse than to be that catatonic coworker propped up on the bar, bloated from too many toddies and pigs in a blanket. Resist the urge to overindulge.

Following are a few more tips on suitable behavior at a holiday office party.

+ **Be tasteful, not tacky.** The office party is a social extension of your business day. The way we dress is the number one indicator of how we value ourselves and the corporation we represent. If it's not a Halloween party, leave those thigh-high disco boots at home!
+ **Toasting.** The host is always the first to toast. If you are being honored with a toast, don't raise your glass, drink, or even clap, as that would mean you are cheering for yourself. You can show your gratitude by making a toast to the person who toasted you. Just be brief, thirty seconds or less, as people's eyes begin to glaze over if you ramble on. This is not just a holiday rule; it should be applied all year long.

- **Don't overindulge.** If you're a big eater, you may want to eat a little something before you leave home. No one will be impressed if you can down more peel-and-eat shrimp than anyone else. Keep drinks to a minimum because "loose lips sink ships." One drink maybe, but two should be the maximum.
- **Keep your dancing PG-rated.** Be sure not to emulate the dance moves you've seen on MTV. Keep it appropriate and do not cross the line. If you are single and find yourself interested in a single coworker, do not pursue that person at the office function. Make plans for another time.
- **Behaving gladly.** Upon arriving, find your hosts and thank them for arranging the party. You also want to say a brief thank-you when you are leaving. If you really want to shine and warm a heart, send a handwritten thank-you note, mentioning the food, location, and your gratitude for a festive and fun evening. It is always best to opt for a handwritten thank-you note as opposed to an e-mailed thank-you note. A handwritten note takes time, shows effort and thought. Just like that, you have arrived, survived, and successfully navigated your holiday office party!

Six

CHILDREN

Lessons from a New York City Cabdriver

The world will reward your children when they display respectful social skills. Several years ago, my husband and I took our children to New York City to live for a month. The exotic foods, diverse cultures, magnificent entertainment, and brilliant architecture were just a few of the wonders that the Big Apple has to offer. Mark Twain said, "Kindness is a language which the deaf can hear and the blind can see." We saw this come true over and over and over again during our stay in New York.

One brisk day we set out for the Metropolitan Museum of Art and hailed a cab. As we climbed in, the cabdriver said, "Good morning. How are you?" Our young sons responded, "Fine, thank you, and how are you?" The cabdriver turned around and looked at my husband and me and said that children rarely spoke to him. The boys went on to tell the cabdriver that we were from Florida, what grades they were in, and other basics. They also asked about the picture of two children on the cabdriver's dashboard. The cabdriver told the boys that his daughters were eight and ten years old, went to school in New Jersey, and were both interested in modern dance and played piano. We all chatted for another five minutes or so until we pulled up to the museum. My husband handed the driver a twenty-dollar bill for the $14.95 fare. The cabdriver turned around, looked back at us, and said, "You all have been so kind to me, there is no charge." Just like that, our children learned the essence of social skills: we experienced an unexpected kindness for showing common courtesy.

HELP YOUR CHILD SHINE!

If your children have a difficult time making eye contact with people, simply have them look for eye color. Then ask them when you walk away, "Didn't that man have beautiful purple eyes?" and your children will glance at you like you've lost your mind and say, "No, Mom, he had blue eyes!" Just like that you've made it fun to learn the basics of eye contact.

Here are a few more steps to help your children shine.

+ When driving to the grocery store, post office, etc., suggest to your children that they say hello as they are looking for the color of people's eyes. If they do say hello while making eye contact, reinforce to them as you walk back to the car, "That was very nice. I'm sure you made her day. Doesn't it feel great to change someone's day?" If they didn't make eye contact or say hello, just say, "I know you can do it, let's practice with the people we meet tomorrow." That's it! No dissertations or lectures, just short and sweet verbal cues.

+ Once you have the eye contact and the hellos down, prompt kids to respond with "Fine, thank you" when someone asks, "How are you?" Again, no lectures when you're walking into the doctor's office, paint store, library, etc. Just give a short verbal cue like this: "When they ask you, 'How are you?' remember to say, 'Fine, thank you.'" The world will reward your child for such a small effort. Even though positive adult reactions are great reinforcement, the best thing is that your child is learning to be socially confident and respectful of others.

+ If having your children chew with their mouth closed seems to be an ongoing battle, make a pact with yourself to catch them doing something good and comment at least three times during dinner or lunch: "Wow, that's great the way you are chewing with your mouth closed," or "I can tell you are getting older by the way you are chewing with your mouth closed more often. *Great job!*" After about seven days of positive verbal cues, the habit should be set.

✦ When it's bedtime and no cell phones, doorbells, or daily tasks are pulling you all over the place, remember to tell your children how they shone that day. Examples: "That was great when you said hello to Mrs. Karalis." "I really appreciated your help bringing in and putting away the groceries." "I'm grateful you used nice table manners." "I saw your little sister trying to chew with her mouth closed because she was watching you."

PLAY DATES: HOST AND GUEST RESPONSIBILITIES

An invitation for a play date should come via the host. If you host a play date, the visiting child's parent does the dropping off and picking up.

Following is some play-date protocol.

✦ Make sure the play date is kept to ninety minutes for four years of age and under and no longer than two hours for older children, unless it's a sleepover.

✦ Be prompt when dropping off and picking up your child. Being on time is important because the host child will be looming by the door in anticipation. Picking up on time is equally important as the host may have plans or it may be nap time for the child and/or mommy. If you are hosting, be sure to reiterate that the pickup time is firm, explaining, "We have a doctor's appointment this afternoon."

✦ Teach your child arrival and departure basics, such as answering the door with a welcoming hello, walking friends to the door when they are leaving, and thanking them for coming. If your children are too small to do this, then model the behavior and say this is what we do when friends visit and go home.

- ✦ Leave your number if dropping off and ask if you can pick up anything for the host while you are out.
- ✦ Bring a healthy snack for the children to share. Remind the host of any allergies, phobias, or make-believe friends your child has.
- ✦ Be sure to teach your child to say "Mr. and Mrs. [Last Name]" unless the hosts have specified they prefer to be called a different or more casual name.
- ✦ Go over the "how to be a polite guest" rules: Thank the host as soon as you arrive, and keep your magic words out in the open: *please* and *thank you* go a long way. After

playing with something, help put it away. Don't run in the house or put your feet on the furniture. Use your library voice, even if you are playing Decibel Man in your pretend play. If you are outside, then you are allowed to let your outside voice boom.

+ If hosting guests, help your child with host duties. Your company are the guests of honor and will get to go first, have their choice of available toys to play with, and also get to choose and open their snack first. If your child has a special toy that is difficult to share, put it away before the play date.

+ If your child is sick, reschedule the play date.

+ When you return home from the play date, have your children draw a picture of something they did. Nothing is better than a stick figure drawn by a child. If you have a minute, send it as a thank-you for the play date. Or you can phone or e-mail a thank-you and schedule a time for you to host a play date for the other child or say that you would like to organize one in a couple of weeks.

SLEEPOVERS

Sleepovers are a rite of passage, filled with excitement and fun, *and* they offer wonderful opportunities for teaching your child the basics of how to be a great host and guest.

For the Host Parent

Share your plans with the parents of your guests before the event. Tell them what you will be serving to eat and the activities you are planning, such as going to the movies, ice-skating, etc. Clearly state pickup and drop-off times and suggest what to bring—for instance, a sleeping bag, flashlight, any medications, and sources of comfort, such as a favorite teddy bear.

Here are several more tips.

- Have two information cards representing each guest: one for the parents to take with them and the second for you to keep.
- On the outgoing card, share vital information, starting with your cell phone and house phone numbers. Also, a soft schedule of the sleepover agenda, such as swimming at two o'clock, dinner at five, movies at seven, and bedtime at eleven. You will want to include the morning pickup time as well. The parents will have a sense of order and safety when you provide this information.
- The second information card is for the parents to leave with you, containing their vital information, starting with the parents' and child's names, and their cell phone and home phone numbers. They should include any allergies to food and pets, and if their child has any habits the parents might want to share, such as waking in the night, sleepwalking, or bed-wetting. It's a good idea for them to jot down any instructions if medications are to be taken.
- Find out if the parents will be picking their child up or if you should expect to see Grandma, another relative, or a friend.
- Have older children give their cell phones to the host parent, for safekeeping and also so the children can focus on the party, not texting.
- Ask parents if they would like their child to call them at bedtime to say good-night.
- As soon as the children arrive, show them the three places they will be spending most of their time, starting with the sleeping area. Help them roll out their sleeping bag and settle their things. This way, their place is set up and you will not need to introduce it as the children prepare for bedtime, when the kids are tired and emotions are fragile. Also, show them the bathrooms and the kitchen, explaining to them what they have access to. Example: "Here are the water bottles on the second shelf on the right. Please help yourself when you get thirsty."

- Once all the sleepover guests have arrived, conduct a short "meeting." Ask if they have any questions or concerns. The children won't have any, as they just want to get the party started. But the mini three-minute meeting is for you to share the three most important house rules: (1) Bedtime. Say something like "Okay, I just want to share that lights are out at eleven P.M. (2) We will show respect to each other, never leaving anyone out. (3) Have fun!"
- A craft might be a great and fun addition. Example: Give the kids pillowcases to decorate with fabric markers. Have all the children sign each pillowcase and include the date of the party. The pillowcase can be used to take home anything they received at the party and can also be the party favor.

For the Guest

- Pack everything that will be needed: toothpaste, toothbrush, clean clothes, pajamas, a flashlight, medications, pillow, sleeping bag, and a snack big enough for everyone to share, such as a box of popcorn. Give it to the parents when you arrive at the party.
- The most important thing to remember to pack is your best manners. Thank the host parent and the child who invited you as soon as you arrive.
- Ask where to put your things and keep them all in one place, not in different areas of the house.
- When using the bathroom, keep it tidy by flushing the toilet, wiping out the sink, and placing your toothbrush and toothpaste in a plastic bag and taking them back to your sleeping area. Also, keep your clothes and anything else you've brought in one location.
- Be a fun part of the party. Include everyone, participate in the activities, and observe the house rules, including any rules about electronics—for example, television, iPods, handheld games, and computers—and bedtime.

- Help clean up each area that has been played in before you move on to the next activity.
- Respect the house and its occupants by not being too loud, not roughhousing, not abusing the furnishings (e.g., don't put your feet on the furniture).
- Have your things packed and ready to go at the scheduled time. Look around and see if anything needs to be picked up, and triple-check that you have all your things together.
- When leaving, thank your friend and his or her parents for inviting you. Let them know how much fun you had.

CHILDREN'S BIRTHDAY PARTIES: GUEST AND HOST RESPONSIBILITIES

For the Guest

Make sure you arrive on time at a child's birthday party. If you are staying with your child at the party, ask the host how you can help. If you aren't staying, thank the host for inviting your child and leave your cell number. Have the number written down so the host doesn't have to look for pen and paper. Before leaving, reconfirm the pickup time.

Following are more children's birthday party tips.

- Ask your child if she remembers the three basic rules of being a great houseguest: (1) Help clean up their plate, napkin, and cup. (2) Be respectful of the house by not running inside, not putting their feet on the furniture, and putting back whatever they play with. (3) Chew with their mouth closed, and don't eat their cake until the birthday child starts eating cake first.
- Make sure your child is confident and assured with her greeting upon arrival, and a "Thank you," looking the adult in the eyes, upon departure. These skills will carry your children through a multitude of social stages, occasions, and parties. So have them practice often.

- The best way to arm your children with these simple social skills is to ask questions and have short dialogues with them about what to do upon arriving at a party and when leaving. Here is an example: "Kristin, why do you think we should always find the host and guest of honor, such as the mom and the birthday child, to say hello to when we arrive?" Let your child tell you the answer, so she understands the reasoning and is not just listening to you chant a bunch of rules. You don't want to sound like Charlie Brown's teacher: "Wah wah wah wah wah wah!" After your child answers your question, repeat what she said. "Yes, Kristin, you got it! Mrs. Kaufmann and little camper will be pleased we've arrived and will be so happy we are there to celebrate with them."

- The appropriate amount to spend on a gift for a child's birthday varies around the country. Around $20 is the average, but it's important to learn what's customary where you live. As in any gift-giving situation, if you can't afford the "going rate," just give what you can. Make sure you attach a card with your name, so the parents and child will know whom the gift is from.

- Thoughtfulness is more important than how much you spend.

- Gift ideas:

  - iTunes card
  - Books
  - Movie theater tickets
  - DVDs
  - Board games
  - LEGO
  - Gift cards to favorite stores

For the Host

If you're hosting a birthday party for your child, here are a few things to keep in mind as you celebrate with your child, family, and their friends.

+ When sending invitations, be sure to put the time, date, location, response date, and a number or RSVP e-mail on the card.
+ If the party *has* to start at a certain time, such as a party at a movie theater, write 1:45 for a 2:00 P.M. movie, so everyone is together and seated at the start of the movie.
+ If you prefer to have just children attend the party, make sure the invitation says drop-off and pickup times. If the entire family can attend the party, address the invitation to the Davis Family.
+ It is perfectly okay to call a person who hasn't replied to your invitation. Just simply call and say, "I'm trying to get a final count for the cupcakes, pizzas, nerve pills, etc. Is Bobby planning to attend?"
+ The golden rule of a birthday party (or any party) is to always buy extra. There will be parents, siblings, and unexpectedly hungry and thirsty birthday attendees. You can always use the additional napkins, plates, water, cups, etc.; they won't go to waste. So prepare for more than you think you will need.
+ Don't feel obligated to give out elaborate goody bags. It's not the Oscars, so no need to send the attendees away with swag bags. You can if you want to, but it's optional. Be mindful that a bulging goody bag with a value higher than some of the gifts might cause hurt feelings.
+ Decide in advance whether your child will open gifts at the party or afterward, considering your child's age and the number of people attending. It's difficult for twenty five-year-olds to sit still while gift after gift is being opened. Etiquette these days suggests opening gifts privately up to the age of ten.
+ Make sure the little guest of honor (birthday child) knows how to greet and thank his or her guests for coming. Short role-playing and/or interactive dialogues are best to teach this skill, thirty seconds at most. Use found time in the car, or anywhere there is lag time. Example: Greeting—"Hello,

Kristin, I'm so happy you are here." Saying good-bye—
"Thank you for coming to my birthday party and also for
the gift."

+ If your child is going to open gifts at the party, make sure
to teach him or her ahead of time a few things about
receiving gifts. Your child should understand the difference
between a polite and an impolite response ("Yuck, I hate
brown socks!") and should be told to say "Thank you" for
each and every gift. Role-play with your child and make it
fun. Draw a picture of an awful gift (say, a bag of Brussels
sprouts) and have fun role-playing, unwrapping the gift
and politely saying, "Thank you, Aunt Gertie," throwing
in something nice about the gift, "Brussels sprouts are the
coolest color of green," and showing how the clueless Aunt
Gertie feels appreciated.

BACK-TO-SCHOOL SUCCESS

As teachers, students, and parents make their way to school on the
first day of the year, remember that emotions are running high
for everyone involved. Some are excited; others are apprehensive.
Below are some suggestions to smooth the transition from
summer to school for all ages, ranks, and personalities.

+ Do a test run. Map out how long it takes to get to school.
Pick up a schedule and do a walk-through of your child's
day. Locate the library, lunchroom, restrooms, etc. Find
the child's locker and practice using the lock.

+ Don't skip open house. The teachers and support staff have
spent hours mapping out a route for your child's success, so
jump on board.

+ Keep your emotions in check on the first day of school. No
hanging around and going into an ugly cry when it's time
to say good-bye to your child. Save your tears for your
friends at Starbucks. A simple and brief good-bye is best.

- ✦ Make the most out of back-to-school shopping. We all know you could buy a small island near Fiji with what you shell out for school clothes and supplies, so you might as well make an adventure out of it. Take just one child at a time and turn shopping into Mommy or Daddy one-on-one time before the summer ends.
- ✦ Don't forget the importance of parent-teacher conferences. Even if you're sitting on small chairs, you can ask big questions. The parent-teacher conference is like a business

meeting, so dress in a respectful manner. Go in prepared with open-ended questions and take notes on what the teacher shares with you.

+ Don't create a logjam during school dismissal. The car line is for picking up, not for giving tests or science-fair explanations. If you have to ask the teacher a question that requires more than a ten-second answer, e-mail her or schedule a conference.

+ Communicate often and early with the teacher. Let her know about your child's interests, allergies, test anxieties, etc. If your child blows up like a float at the Macy's parade after exposure to nuts, the drop-off line on the first day of school is not the time to alert the teacher.

+ Start school rituals seven to fourteen days before school starts. Have your children do dry runs of laying out their clothes and preparing lunches, as well as implementing the "back-to-school bedtime drill," so they can adapt their internal clock to school wake-up hours.

+ Don't let backpacks and lunch boxes ferment in your hundred-degree SUV. When you get home from school, have the kids clean them out and hang them up before they hunker down to enjoy their afternoon snacks.

+ Don't forget to put your child's teacher on a pedestal. They are building the childhood hopes and the academic health of your little one, so be supportive, ask them how you can help, and find out what they need. If they ask you for a kidney—*give it to them.*

SPORTSMANSHIP

Both parents and children should be good sports in any type of competitive situation. The parents' actions and attitudes mold a child's sportsmanship IQ. So be at your best when coaching, refereeing, and watching your child's play. Show support for the officials no matter what.

Here are a few more tips on teaching children about good sportsmanship.

- ✦ If you shout, let it be words of encouragement. Be considerate of other players, their families, and the opposing team.
- ✦ Follow the rules. No explanation needed.
- ✦ Don't argue with your coach, teammates, umpires, or referees. Show respect and support to the entire cast of the game. If you do have a point to share or a genuine disagreement, present it with decorum and brevity.
- ✦ Thank your teammates, your coaches, the scorekeepers, the manager, and the players on the other team. Shake hands at the end of the game and find a way to throw in an "I appreciate the time and effort you gave to our team."
- ✦ Keep your perspective. Sports can teach your child so many things, including that winning isn't the only acceptable outcome. Really! A good attitude is an important life skill. So talk about the plays, the surprising moves, and any improvements that might assist in the next game.
- ✦ Use professional sports to help you teach your child. Talk about the choices professional athletes make and the tone they set. Point out examples of good sportsmanship in professional athletes and talk about the unfortunate choices as well. Ask your child if watching rude and unsportsmanlike behavior makes them trust and like an athlete or leaves them with a bad feeling. Be careful not to impose your opinion on your child; just share the tone such behavior sets in the media. It is almost always true that the most respectful players get the biggest endorsement deals. That can teach a nice connection between being respectful and reaping big dividends.
- ✦ Be a gracious winner. Be humble while being grateful. Thank the losing team for a good game. Tip your hat, shake hands, and say you're looking forward to playing the team in the next game.

- ✦ Be a gracious loser. Losing is part of the game. Know that when you lose, a win can be just around the corner. With a positive attitude, thank the winning team for a good game, while making a specific comment about their strategy or a particular play and offering a handshake.
- ✦ Don't forget to enjoy the game. Teach your child to take

the best out of both winning and losing and apply it to future games and competitive situations.

GHOULISHLY GOOD MANNERS FOR HALLOWEEN

As the nights grow cooler and the leaves begin to change colors, images of ghosts, goblins, and pirates begin to dance in the minds of the youthful, playful, and young at heart. What will you dress up as for Halloween? On the outside, you may plan to morph into your favorite superhero, cartoon character, or fairy-tale princess, but don't forget to bring your ladylike or gentlemanly manners along with you. Even monsters know the importance of good manners.

Below are some tips for this fun-filled spooky night.

+ The number-one rule is no light, no knock. If you ignore this rule and knock anyway, knock only once. That goes for doorbells, too.
+ Always say "Trick or treat" and no greedy grabbing. If people leave a bowl of candy out with the sign PLEASE TAKE ONLY ONE, they trust you. Show that you are trustworthy and follow the honor code.
+ Always say "Thank you" after you have gotten your treat.
+ Stay on sidewalks; it is not polite to trample on people's lawns.
+ Try to wrap up your trick-or-treating by 9:00 to 9:30 P.M., as your youngest trick-or-treaters must get ready for bed.

The Ungraciousness Bag

A tip for the adults on Halloween: have an "ungraciousness bag." If your kids greedy-grab, forget to say thank you, run through lawns, knock too many times, or play unkind tricks on siblings and neighbors, have them donate a few pieces of their candy to your ungraciousness bag. The bag also doubles as a safety bag to hold your bug spray, cell phone, water, and flashlight.

SOCIAL ETIQUETTE AND RESPECT FOR OTHERS

Any child who knows these basics will have a leg up on behaving appropriately in social settings.

+ Elbows off the table unless it's between courses or after dessert. This helps with posture, too. Sitting upright sends a silent message of respect for self and others; slouching, which is becoming universal, sends the opposite message. Tell your kids that gravity doesn't need any help holding the table down, so arms off the table. Having nice posture gives an impression of strength, confidence, and capability.
+ A napkin isn't a flag of surrender. Teach children it isn't intended for washing their face, just dabbing. Napkins are not for blowing your nose, either. Just let it rest in the lap and not on the shirt like a bib. Never put the napkin on a plate when finished eating; always put it on the table to the left of the plate.
+ Wait until everyone has been served before you start eating. When the host picks up his or her fork or gives a verbal okay, it's time to eat.
+ Pass food to the right and never reach over others to serve yourself. Try all foods, and use positive words about what you've been served. Pace yourself with the other diners, not eating too fast or too slow.
+ When finished with your meal, wait a few minutes, then ask to be excused. Clear your place and ask how you might help with after-dinner cleanup. It's important to thank the host, even if it's your mom or dad, and try to say one specific nice thing when doing the thanking. Example: "I loved the potatoes tonight, they were extra crunchy."
+ Be a secret agent and search for treasures. Treasures are tiny

facts about other people, details that make a person unique and that matter to that individual. Find out a person's favorite color, ball team, or holiday memory. Explain to your child this is to keep from talking too much about herself. Treasure-hunting is a wonderful way to learn about others and build friendships. It shouldn't be an interrogation, but a two-way interaction to share interests.

✦ Set a goal of one act of kindness a week. For example, bake cookies for a neighbor. Deliver the cookies while they are still warm and just like that an act of kindness has been done. Bring a neighbor's trash can up from the road, or pick up trash that a litterbug has discarded. Keep a chart. It's amazing how good the kids will feel learning to put other people first without the expectation of notice.

✦ Get grunt work out of the way first. Teach your children to delay gratification in a world of increasingly instantaneous pleasure. Do the big job first (say, raking all the leaves), and save painting the mailbox (the fun thing) for last. The fun thing will be enjoyed so much more when children know no bigger, dreaded job is waiting for them. Teaching them this will help equip them with great homework and time-management skills.

✦ Basic greetings go a long way. People need to be acknowledged and recognized. We all want to feel as if we matter. So the most basic greeting of "Hello, Mrs. Sumpter" to the preschool teacher will win social points for your child right from toddlerhood.

✦ My grandmother drilled into me, "Gossip makes you ugly!" so gossiping was always unappealing no matter how alluring the tidbit itself seemed. Teach your children that gossiping might make you feel good for a moment, but it will leave a trail of dread and hurt feelings. Here are some ways to avoid gossip: (1) Role-play with your kids to teach them how to change the subject when they smell gossip, or even how to excuse themselves with an upbeat "It was great catching up with you, but I forgot to turn in my homework.

See you later." (2) They could use the direct approach—"Let's not talk about Stephanie; she's not here to defend herself." (3) Try the funny approach—"I have way too much to fix in myself to spend time talking about Susie." Your children should know that a gossiper will always make *you* a topic of conversation at some point. Teach them that they aren't exempt and to be wise judges of character: a gossiper may not be the best choice for a friend.

THANK-YOU NOTES YOUR KIDS WILL LOVE WRITING

The number-one way to get your children to write thank-you notes for the gifts they have received is to have them write the notes before they get to smell, paw, or glance too long at the newly opened gift. Simply say, "Once you write the thank-you note to Aunt Joy for the LEGOs, you may play with the gift." I love this rule since my kids chase me around saying, "Here is my thank-you note. Now may I open my LEGOs?"

Here are a few more tips.

+ Give children the option to write with many colored markers or just a simple blue- or black-ink pen. Children almost always choose the color option and will enjoy the task more if they can be creative with their thank-you notes. Introduce a variety of stamps as well and take your kids to the post office to pick them out. Choose stamps that the recipients might like, such as sports, comics, famous artists, etc.
+ Offer stationery that is fun, colorful, and reflects your child's interests. If they are into lizards, pink horses, or watermelon patches, buy notes decorated with them. Designate a special drawer or cabinet for thank-you notes so the kids know exactly where to find them and aren't stalking you for paper, envelopes, and stamps.

- Empower them by starting the habit of always being courteous. If they are too small to write sentences, get the fill-in-the-blank thank-you notes or have them draw a picture and you can write on the picture, "Harrison loved his gift."
- Teach them the 444 Rule: Write at least four lines, take about four minutes, and mail within four days of receiving the gift.
- Let your children express themselves. If they want to draw a picture of the New York Yankees PR marketing guy with the spiked hair while thanking him for the Yankees tickets, let them. Don't worry about fixing spelling errors or make them correct backward letters. Nothing is more special than receiving a thank-you note in an innocent child's writing.
- A few days before a party, remind kids that they must write their thank-you notes before playing with their gifts.
- Take ten seconds before the party kicks off to again remind your child of the thank-you note procedure; overstimulated children full of cake and sugar might spontaneously combust or have selective memory the day of the party. Remind them to (1) write a thank-you for each gift; (2) address each envelope; (3) place a stamp on each envelope; and (4) place the notes in the mailbox.

PETIQUETTE

What I Learned from Jack

When I was a little girl, we adopted our dog from what was called the dog pound (now called the SPCA) in North Carolina. The previous owner of this adorable mixed-shepherd breed had named him Jack Daniels. Jack was my favorite topic. I could never figure out why my Sunday-school teacher's brow furrowed each time I mentioned Jack Daniels in front of the class. My mortified grandmother would always say, "Patricia Ann, we don't need to use Jack's surname. His first name is just fine."

Childhood pets are one of the best parts of childhood. The next time you are at a party, steer the conversation toward the animals people had as children and watch people's eyes light up. Dogs have the best manners. They always stand when we walk into a room, giving us a greeting suited for a diplomat. They are loyal, never gossip, never hold grudges, and forgive us the instant we step on their toes or tail. They show real sadness when we depart, even if it's just to walk to the mailbox. They fiercely protect us despite our dressing them up in undignified costumes for neighborhood parades. No wonder millionaires will their entire estates to their beloved pets.

Following are some guidelines for living day to day and traveling with our furry friends.

THE DOG PARK

Before you head out the door to the dog park with your precious pooch, make sure your pet has had a thorough checkup and gotten a green light from the vet. Also do a drive-by and check out the puppy recreation area solo and become accustomed with the rules and flow of the playing field before letting loose your beloved canine.

Here are more tips so both you and your dog have a great playtime together.

✦ When you arrive, be calm; dogs can always sense your energy. When you enter and exit the gate, make sure it is closed securely behind you. Totally unplug: this isn't the

time to be talking on your phone, texting, or surfing the Web. Don't wear headphones or listen to music. It's important to keep your eyes on your pet the entire time you're visiting the dog park.

+ Don't dress your pet in a costume of any kind, even if it's Halloween. The garments could get caught on exposed fencing or excite or confuse other dogs. Your pet should wear an everyday collar with tags; don't outfit it with choke chains or vanity or spiked collars, as these can endanger your dog and other pets playing in the dog park.

+ Keep a close eye on dogs when they are playing, making sure there's no aggressive, rough play. Make sure they aren't digging, chewing, or jumping on other people. If they do dig a hole, cover it up ASAP, so no one will twist an ankle. If dogs are acting aggressively, take them home. It isn't fair to your dog or the other dogs visiting the park, and you don't want to break up or be the cause of a dogfight.

+ If your dog is ill, don't expose healthy pets to it. If the dog has fleas, mange, or a runny nose or eyes, plan a trip to the vet and not the dog park. Never let your dog share a communal water bowl. Bring a separate bowl for your dog and fill it up at the park.

+ Follow the rules of the dog park. Number one should be pick up after your dog. Bags should be available, but always bring your own just in case and discard solid waste properly.

+ If your dog is in heat, never take her to the dog park and expose her to unneutered males.

+ Be careful when taking children to dog parks. If children are under ten, think twice about taking them to the puppy playground. If you do take your child, limit their running, skipping, and yelling, as those are invitations to play rough and chase. Avoid any rough playing and/or sudden movements. Refrain from hugging, squeezing, and petting other dogs. Always ask the owner if it's permissible to touch their pet.

PETS AND TRAVEL

HOSTING A GUEST WHEN YOU HAVE A PET

+ Before your get-together, share with your guests that you have dogs, cats, etc. The guests can then let you know if they are allergic, afraid, or uncomfortable with animals.

+ Scoop the poop. Even though poop helps the environment and enhances the greenness of your lawn and the lawn of your neighbor, the smell and sight kind of outweigh the benefits. So go ahead, do the right thing, stoop and scoop, so your yard and surrounding yards are clean and pristine.

+ Pet hair. It's difficult to look professional, neatly put together, and polished with a gob of hair hitching a ride on your new black pants. Try your best to keep your home, office, and car interior free of pet hair. It's one accessory your friends and coworkers can do without. They may love Fido as much as you do, but they probably don't want that hair ball as a parting gift.

+ Guests get the seat of honor! People should get the seats in your home or office, not pets. I've seen people standing at parties because the host's beloved Coco was spread-eagled on the sofa. Let people eat their Brie in peace, not being sniffed, nudged, and jumped on for a bite of food. I once had to crawl under my host's computer desk just to eat my chocolate mousse in peace. Until Poochie is properly trained, he should catch a nap and spend quality time in his crate or another part of your home when you are entertaining.

+ Think of others first. We know Sparky is a part of your color wheel, but try to remember that some people are frightened by or have phobias or allergies to dogs, cats, and lizards. If a cacophony of barks, jumps, slobbery licks, and sniffing is coupled with your chanting, "Get down!" as guests arrive, it might be best to do the greeting outside or put Sparky in a safe place.

- Puppy obedience training is a great solution for socializing your pet with other animals and people. Your dog will learn basic commands that will eliminate most puppy behavior problems. If you are planning on having a large number of people over, it may be overwhelming or overstimulating for your dog, so try to have realistic expectations.
- Save the pet tricks for *David Letterman*. Please refrain from making your sweet pooch perform trick after trick for your visitors. Do one or two tricks at the most. More than that and people are just pretending to be intrigued.
- One picture of Fifi or Fido in your wallet or on your desk is plenty.

TRAVELING WITH PETS

- Call your hotel or browse its Web site before you depart to find out its pet policy. Never bring a pet to a friend's house without clearing it with them first.
- Bring along your pet's favorite toys, blankets, food, and dishes for a higher comfort level when you are traveling. Pack enough food as it isn't a good idea to change their food when traveling. It could upset the pet's stomach.
- Also bring along your pet's documented health history, updated medical records, medicines, and supplements. The medical records and documents should store easily on your laptop or icloud.com. It might be a good idea to pack a picture of your pet just in case it gets lost. Don't forget your pet first-aid kit. It should contain antibiotic cream, bandages, and tweezers.
- Have your pet groomed before you travel! He will feel better and so will you and your travel mates. You don't want Skippy to be nicknamed Stinky by the people you come in contact with. Remember to tip the groomer 15 to 20 percent. Your pet must go to the vet for a good checkup and to make sure all records are up-to-date before you depart.

- Request the ground floor of hotels. This provides easier access to the outdoors for bathroom breaks and walks.
- Leaving your beloved pooch in the hotel room alone is strongly discouraged, as the housekeeping staff may become alarmed. If you do have to leave your pet in the room, make sure he is comfortably crated and has new and interesting chew toys. Leave the radio or TV on to keep him company. Let the desk clerk know you are stepping out, and leave your cell number in case the hotel needs to reach you.
- Feed your pet in the bathroom to keep the carpet clean and free from spilled water and food. Also bring light towels or sheets to cover the furniture or anywhere your pet might lie down.
- Make sure you pack your pet's "petiquette." He must be house-trained, not chewing up everything in sight, jumping, scratching, digging, and running around knocking things over, before you "unleash" him on the world.

VISITING OTHERS WITH YOUR PETS

- Pack a bag for your pet. Pack your pet's favorite things: treats, two or three favorite toys, his most comfortable blanket. Make sure to pack a lint brush. If you will be staying for an extended time, take along the pet's crate and an extra leash and collar. Let your pet see and smell his puppy bag and its contents for a few days before you leave. The smells and physical treasures from home will help comfort your pet on the road. Don't forget favorite foods: changing a pet's food mid-stay can cause stomach problems.
- Even if you are staying for only one night, make sure you have all your pet's medical and vaccination records and tags. Have two forms, one scanned to your computer and one physical copy. Let your host know how to access these in case of an emergency. Also, let your vet and a few friends know where you will be traveling in case they get a call from your host.

- A nice touch when visiting a friend or family with pets is to bring a small gift for your host's pet: the newest fun chew toy, a soft pet blanket, or small, all-natural pet treats. Present the pet gift to your host, and let them determine when to give it to their pet.

- To ensure that your pet will be a gracious guest, make sure it has three simple skills down pat: how to sit, stay, and lie down. These skills will guarantee your pet stays close to you and doesn't roam the house unattended. Keep your pet in sight at all times. Even the most well-trained and trusted pet can veer off course in a new environment.

- Slowly introduce your pet to any resident pets. Be careful to do it with ease and grace, not in a rush. A walk might be the perfect solution to let pets get acquainted with one another. Never leave them alone until you see how they will get along.

- The sofa, chairs, beds, and any other furniture is off-limits. Make sure some pet toys are out for chewing, and be mindful to prevent excessive jumping on and licking of your host.

- When taking your pet out to do its business, make sure to pick up and discard the waste properly. Don't even try that bend-and-pretend routine. It's your obligation to clean up your pet's waste, so pick it up. Ask your host the best place to dispose of your pet's waste, and also any house rules that the host's pet follows.

- Always write a thank-you note and send a host gift, maybe flowers, chocolates, or a book about the hosts' breed of dog. Thank them for a wonderful time, brag about their well-behaved pet, and mention one or two favorite things or memories.

VISITING THE VETERINARIAN'S OFFICE

Visiting the vet's office doesn't have to be stressful for you or your pet if you follow a few simple steps. Start with picking up the phone and making an appointment. Don't assume the vet is available to see you and your pet anytime. Schedule an appointment and do the following:

+ If at all possible, leave the children behind. Get a sitter for the kids. Focus on your pet and on asking the vet for information. Also, the children will be safer out of the way of unfamiliar or ill animals.
+ Be sure to carry small animals in a pet carrier. Dogs should remain on a short leash.
+ Have pets do their business before you get into the office. If your pet has an accident indoors, let someone on staff know and offer to clean it up.
+ If you are visiting a new vet, bring any relevant medical records with you to give to the new office staff.
+ While waiting in the reception area, keep your pet close at your side and do not let him wander around the office or walk up to people and other pets.
+ No need to put your furry friend on the table in the exam room until the vet arrives, then be sure to hold the pet. Do not walk away assuming he will stay up on the table unattended.
+ Turn all cellular devices to silent mode or, better yet, don't bring them in with you.
+ Don't talk when the vet has the stethoscope in his ears. Wait patiently until he is finished, then ask your questions. Be sure to let the vet know of any recent changes in your pet's health or behavior.
+ Direct your questions and concerns to the doctor. Don't baby-talk to your pet about his symptom-wymptoms.
+ Pay close attention to the vet's plan of treatment; write down all instructions and follow them exactly.
+ If you have to leave your pet at the vet's office for a procedure or board him for a trip, be sure the office has your current phone numbers and an emergency contact. Also, leave your pet's favorite blanket and toy, so he has something from home to comfort him.

You may want to bring some treats to give to your pet for his good behavior at the vet's office and maybe reward yourself with a latte on your way home for your fine conduct as well!

SERVICE ANIMAL ETIQUETTE

Today, many types of animals are trained to assist people with various disabilities. We are most familiar with Seeing Eye dogs, as they were the first, aiding the blind starting in the United States back in 1929. Nowadays, not only are dogs service animals, but also cats, monkeys, horses, potbellied pigs, etc., which are trained to perform specialized duties. In addition to leading the blind or visually impaired, service animals assist the deaf and hearing impaired, provide companionship to the elderly and those with mental and emotional disorders, alert companions to the onset of seizures and diabetes at-

tacks, help with balance, push and pull wheelchairs, open and close doors, turn lights on and off, retrieve items, and even dial 911.

With more and more people assisted by service animals today, the general public needs to know the protocol when encountering these specially trained helpers.

- ✦ Keep in mind that a service animal is not a pet when he is working. He is trained to ignore distractions and be alert to dangers, so respect his position. One way to identify a service animal is to look for a harness or possibly a cape that reads SERVICE ANIMAL.
- ✦ Speak to the handler and not the animal when encountering service pets. That way the animal can stay focused on his responsibilities.
- ✦ Always ask for permission to speak to or to pet the animal, and don't be offended if you are asked not to touch him.
- ✦ Do not call out to or make loud noises that will distract a service animal. Diversions may overrule training and cause obedience problems.
- ✦ Never offer food to service animals. Although they are trained to resist such temptations, this will only make their job more difficult, and they may give in to the offer. You don't want to put their handler's safety at risk and jeopardize the animal's important job.

Service animals are special animals that offer independence to people who might not have such freedom without them. Avoid the temptation to interfere.

CAT OWNER ETIQUETTE

You and your cat probably have very different ideas on the meaning of cat etiquette. Most cats are fairly oblivious to it. As you prepare your guest list for a party, kitty is thinking, "I am about to bring up a hair ball; where is the nearest sofa or Oriental rug?"

Sometimes cats and company don't mix. If you want to ensure

the safety of your cat and the comfort of your guests, here are a few tips.

- Prepare a safe haven for kitty. Put food, water, and a litter box in her place of refuge. Then post a sign on the door stating the cat is inside and does not want to be disturbed. It's probably a good idea to leave the door open a crack, because as soon as you put your friendly feline in that room and close the door, you will hear forepaws hammering away and meows pleading for release. This is just a safe place for kitty if the presence of company becomes overwhelming.

- Find out if any of your guests have cat allergies, and before they arrive, remove all furry fleece from the furniture and vacuum thoroughly. Later, if you see Fluffy heading for the lap of the allergic visitor, as kitties are prone to do, be sure to keep her away.

- Always be aware of where the cat is lurking when people are arriving and leaving. Kitties have an uncanny ability to slip out of doors when no one is looking, or to weave between people's feet as they arrive. Observing Garfield getting stepped on or watching guests tumble down stairs is probably not on the evening's agenda.

- Children tend to want to pet, play with, and hold soft, cuddly creatures. But if your generally lovable feline is unfamiliar with the youngster, claws may come out or ankles might get nipped.

- Make sure your silky feline isn't slinking around where food is being served. The easiest way to make sure Sylvester keeps all four on the floor is to never allow him on tables and counters to begin with, even when guests are not around.

- Have a lint roller available. Your cat will most likely scope out the guest wearing clothes that are a complete contrast to her prized fleece. Visitors probably won't ask for a lint roller, so be ready to offer one if you see they are wearing a new fur coat that strongly resembles your kitty.

♦ Have a fresh bottle of eyewash available should any guest make the mistake of rubbing her eyes after petting Mr. Bigglesworth.

Chances are your sweet kitty will want to stay in its safe haven while company hangs around. But we all know cats have a mind of their own, and when we think we have them figured out, we soon discover that we don't. So always be prepared.

Eight

TRAVEL

What I Learned on a Hot, Stinky Bus in France, and It Had Nothing to Do with Cheese

My grandmother always said the number-one rule of manners is kindness. When she instructed me, I would roll my eyes and day-dream about starched linens, glistening china, and shiny silver. But as always, Grandmother was right.

I grew up in the country, where a big evening event was catching lightning bugs, not going to the theater. Fine dining meant going to the local hospital after church to eat in their cafeteria. I longed to know more, be more, and see more.

In college, I spent a summer studying in Europe. Money was tight, with no room for extras such as the trendy European clothes and fancy meals my friends were buying. I felt embarrassed and awkward. But that soon changed.

My friends and I were on a hot, crowded bus in France with standing room only. The mood was disgruntled at best, and the bus and its passengers seemed to groan in unison with every lurch and stop.

At what seemed like our ninety-ninth stop, an elderly lady boarded the bus. I got up, took her arm, and guided her to my seat. All of a sudden, the whole bus broke out in loud applause and cheering. I looked up to see what all the commotion was about. Smiling back at me were men, women, and children from all different cultures.

With a simple five-second act of kindness, the entire mood of the bus changed from hostile to happy. Yes, Grandmother, you were right. Kindness is the number-one rule of manners, and it transcends every culture and any situation. I learned that day that I had been equipped with treasures that money can't buy. Kindness is truly the universal language.

AIRPLANE / AIRPORT ETIQUETTE

Once you get over the trauma of having to perform an impromptu semi-strip-search at the security gate, regroup and gather your belongings, then prepare to have a pleasant and harmonious flight. With passengers overcrowded in tight spaces, coupled with nerves

TAKE YOUR TIME WHEN BOARDING THE PLANE, BUT DON'T LINGER. CARRY YOUR BAG DIRECTLY IN FRONT OF YOU, NOT SLUNG OVER YOUR SHOULDER.

HELP CHILDREN ENJOY THEIR FLIGHT AND STAY BUSY BY PACKING TOYS, VIDEOS, AND SNACKS.

NEVER PUT BAGGAGE IN THE FRONT OVERHEAD COMPARTMENT IF YOU AREN'T SEATED THERE.

IF YOU FREQUENT THE RESTROOM DURING FLIGHTS, TRY TO BOOK AN AISLE SEAT. BE QUICK AND TIDY WHEN USING THE RESTROOM.

and preflight jitters, the best things you can pack are decorum, humor, and tolerance.

Below are a few tips for respectful airline behavior.

+ Take your time when boarding the plane, but don't linger. Make sure you carry your bag directly in front of you, not slung over your shoulder. Otherwise an unlucky passenger may get sideswiped by your bag.
+ Never, ever put your baggage in the front overhead compartment if you aren't seated there. It is unfair for passengers in front to have to hike to the back of the plane to stow their luggage. They'll want to get off the plane as fast as you do, so it isn't polite to expect them to wait for the entire plane to empty before they can get to the back and retrieve their bags. As a general rule, your bags should be near you at all times, so as not to inconvenience anyone else.
+ To help children and the other passengers enjoy the flight, pack new toys, videos, and snacks to keep the kids busy. It may be a great idea to let your child have one new electronic game per hour of flight. Even special treats they don't normally get will help keep them happy and entertained. One caveat: do not break into them until the flight has taken off, as the child might blow through everything before you've even pushed back from the gate.
+ The middle person in your row has the right to both armrests. Fair and simple! Anyone in that detestable, backbreaking middle seat deserves both armrests!
+ Don't board with pungent foods such as tuna or garlic pasta. Take a small sabbatical from wearing perfume or cologne, as many people are allergic in tight quarters. Also, if you are a smoker, be aware that smoke can linger on your clothing and waft around your companions in flight. Nothing is worse than trying to consume a honey-roasted peanut and having the smell of smoke overpower the taste.
+ Before pushing back in your seat, be considerate. Take a

glace backward and give a verbal cue to the person seated behind you, saying, "May I lean back?" It will save many a laptop and also drinks from spilling all over.

+ If you frequent the restroom during flights, do your best to book an aisle seat so you don't have to do Olympic hurdles over a sleeping seatmate. Keep in mind that the restroom is not a day spa, but a two-by-four-foot space that has to accommodate a large number of people, so be quick and tidy when using it.

+ The seat in front of you isn't for doing chin-ups. Show respect for the person in front of you by refraining from using their seat as a catapult to vault yourself to a standing position.

+ Be watchful in your alcohol consumption. The effects of alcohol are double at high altitudes.

+ The baggage claim isn't shooting out lottery tickets or dates with George Clooney, so back up. Stand at least three feet from the conveyor belt so people can step in to claim their luggage. Don't worry, you'll still see your luggage when it comes around.

BED-AND-BREAKFASTS

A bed-and-breakfast is usually someone's residence as well as their business. Showing respect to the innkeepers and the other patrons ensures a memorable and relaxing time for everybody.

Here's what to keep in mind when visiting a bed-and-breakfast.

+ Keep noise levels low early in the morning and late at night.

+ Knowing the check-in and checkout times helps to maintain the household's natural flow so everything will run more smoothly. Note when breakfast, teas, or any other timed eating arrangements are scheduled and make sure you are on time.

+ Innkeepers have great local knowledge to share, such as

their favorite places to eat, visit, and explore, but be careful not to take up too much of their time. Remember, they have an entire inn to operate.

✦ If you have any special needs such as dietary or physical restrictions, let innkeepers know before your arrival, to make sure they can accommodate you.

✦ Tips are appreciated and should be given at the end of your stay. Enclose the tip with a thank-you note highlighting the three things you most enjoyed about their inn and the surrounding area. Present it to your innkeepers in an envelope as you depart while verbally thanking them.

CAMPING

Camping is the perfect way to get away from the hustle and bustle of everyday life, explore, relax, and soak up the nature around you. Camping has a remarkable way of bringing family and friends closer together. Here are a few simple rules to follow when sharing the environment with fellow campers.

✦ When you pitch your tent, keep it a comfortable distance from those of other guests, especially if twenty acres of space are available. Don't zigzag through anyone else's campsite while on your way around the grounds.

✦ Be respectful of the environment. Keep shrubs, trees, and all other forms of vegetation healthy and thriving. Stick to the hiking trails so you don't trample any of the precious surroundings. Dispose of your biodegradable soapy water, toothpastes, etc., at least a hundred feet away from any natural water source.

✦ Make sure your latrine is a hundred yards away from camp, downstream and downwind. Your friends, family, pets, and fellow campers will appreciate this gesture. Your latrine should be a safe distance from streams, rivers, and lakes, to avoid runoff contamination.

✦ Meet fellow campers by being neighborly. You can offer to

help set up their campsite and share points of interest, such as showers, trails, etc.

✦ Remember, sound carries. Don't trust the thin walls of your tent. Keep your interactions private, and remember that noise echoes triple if you pitched your tent near water. Even whispers can be decoded while camping, so think library voice while talking, laughing, and playing music.

✦ Keep your pets on a six-foot leash to protect the wildlife, other campers, and for your pets' own safety. Be sure to clean up after them; your fellow campers will appreciate it.

✦ Read the campground rules and follow them. Make sure to observe the quiet-time hours, which are usually around ten or eleven P.M. to six A.M. Completely shut down everything—your voices, your electronics, TV, and anything else that makes noise—until curfew has been lifted.

✦ Leave your campsite better than you found it. Whatever you carry in, take back out. Also, search for ways to improve the area—pick up even the smallest trace of litter: cigarette butts, bottle caps, straws, etc.

✦ Be extrasafe and triple-check your fire pit to make sure your bonfire is completely extinguished. Follow the camp's guidelines for safety in putting out a fire.

✦ Share the wealth and leave a note tacked to a tree or secured with a rock on the site's picnic table labeled "Welcome, campers" for the campers who come after you. Inform them of your discoveries, points of interest, best fishing spots, etc. Close with well-wishes for a great time; it only takes a few lines and a few minutes.

CRUISES

A cruise offers every class, culture, and age group the opportunity for an adventure at sea. The collective goal of relaxing, rejuvenating, and refreshing can be experienced only if cruise etiquette is followed at all times. The floating vessel houses hundreds of people in close quarters just like an airplane, so make sure the top three things you pack are your best soft social skills, discernment, and a sense of humor.

Below are some tips to make your cruise a delightful experience.

+ Take the time to research what type of cruise would fit your interests and lifestyle: adventure, educational, romantic, singles, family; the choices are endless.
+ Remember three words when packing for your cruise: *modesty, comfort,* and *elegance.* Be sure to refer to your cruise line for suggestions and guidelines.
+ Trust the system. Follow the rules for embarkation, debarkation, customs, and provisions. The cruise personnel and their support staff have it down to a science.
+ Do what's right in tipping. Ask your onboard concierge or go to www.cruisetip.tpkeller.com for proper gratuity distribution. Some cruise lines factor in tips with your ticket, but many do not, so budget accordingly.
+ Don't place more than three servings of food on your plate at the buffet. You can make as many trips as you please to the smorgasbord, so don't pile on the food as if you are on the *Titanic* and it's the last supper.
+ Try to use the stairs. Elevators usually have long lines, and walking will help keep you in shape. If you do use the elevators, let people get off before you try to enter.
+ Pack important things in your carry-on: laptop, camera, passport, jewelry, change of clothes, medications, toothbrush, three ounces of toothpaste, iPod, smartphone, and anything else you can't live without.
+ Be sure to make three copies of your airline and cruise ticket, passport/visa, and itinerary. Place one in your carry-on, another in your checked luggage, and the third at home. You can also scan the documents and e-mail them to yourself or to your icloud account so you can access them from any computer away from home.

- Do your excursion homework. Excursions can sometimes be costly. Call or visit the local sources in each port and ask their advice on reputable, economical excursion alternatives.
- Take the time to read the cruise news that is slipped under your door nightly. It highlights everything you'll want to know, from the next day's weather, to activities, games, excursions, local shopping deals, closures, and much more.
- Make yourself comfortable with the easiest way to navigate the ship. Find the most important areas as soon as you board, such as the spa, dining room, and pool. Figure out the best route to and from your cabin while visiting those areas.
- Don't call it a boat; it's a ship and it's a *she*, not a *he*. Don't forget your basic nautical terms. Port is the left side, starboard is the right side, bow is the front, and stern is the back.
- Do not skip the lifeboat drill. The safety demonstration is not a time to make jokes about the orange life vest clashing with the color of your outfit. Pay attention—it could save your life.
- Don't sleep late if you plan on having a great seat by the pool. Early risers get the coveted poolside loungers.
- Don't be a cruise stalker. It's okay to meet your new friend for a swim or a game of poker, but don't latch on to them for the entire trip.
- Don't wear jeans on formal night even if you paid $350 for them.
- Don't ask to speak to the captain if you have a problem. The cruise personnel have competent officers and crew members to deal with all situations.
- Don't forget to pack an extra collapsible bag to bring home the treasures you'll collect on your odyssey at sea.
- Don't be known as the Decibel King or Queen. Keep your voice low in your room and also in the halls while going to your room. Sound carries on ships.

- Don't skip dinner on your last night to avoid tipping the headwaiter and waitstaff. You want to honor the people who have worked hard to give you great service and also give them a proper good-bye.
- Don't forget to write a note of thanks to the people who have worked hard to make your trip wonderful. Put the note in with your tip.

HOTELS

Whether you are there for business or pleasure, you must adhere to a hotel's code of behavior. Following are some guidelines to keep in mind.

- When navigating your way through a resort hotel, the first people you are going to see are the parking valets. You tip them when they return your car and not upon arrival. A standard tip is two to three dollars.
- Next you are going to notice the bellmen. They take your luggage from your car to the front desk, then to your room. A standard gratuity is about $1 per bag, unless you pack that big ol' backbreaker. Then you'll want to give them a little more.
- The front desk's main goal is to check you in with ease and grace. Though of course you can give them your name, it's a bonus if you have your reservation number.
- Concierges can help you with simple things, such as restaurant recommendations and directions. They can also help you get tickets to the theater or to a sporting event. The standard gratuity is around three to five dollars for each reservation or other assistance. If they go above and beyond and get you a table at a restaurant that's impossible to get into, or tickets to a sold-out baseball game, the gratuity should be around ten to twenty dollars.
- Housekeeping management aspires to make your home away from home as enjoyable as possible. They supply you

REMEMBER TO TIP THE PARKING VALETS, THE BELLMAN, AND THE HOUSEKEEPERS. THEIR AIM IS TO MAKE YOUR VISIT AS ENJOYABLE AS POSSIBLE.

THE FRONT DESK IS A GREAT SOURCE OF HOTEL KNOWLEDGE, BUT SEE THE CONCIERGE FOR VITAL INFORMATION.

WHETHER YOUR STAY IS FOR BUSINESS OR PLEASURE, ALWAYS ADHERE TO THE HOTEL'S CODE OF BEHAVIOR.

CHECK OUT HANDS-FREE AND STRESS-FREE BY HAVING THE VALET BRING YOUR CAR AROUND AND ASKING THE BELLMAN TO DELIVER YOUR LUGGAGE.

with all the extras: extra toiletries, more towels, pillows, and blankets. The standard gratuity is around one dollar per item.

✦ Room attendants/housekeepers are the professionals who keep your room fresh, nice, and clean. They are not your mama, so don't leave your clothes all over the place. Help them keep it neat and nice. I know when I get back to my room and the bed is made and it is clean, I want to give them one of my kidneys! But you don't have to go that far. Standard is two to five dollars per day, and you can leave it in an envelope on the pillow or by the sink in the bathroom. You want to do that daily if possible so it gets to the right person.

+ When getting ready to check out, take an extra two to three minutes to call down to the valet to have your car brought around, then be connected with the bellman to have your luggage retrieved; you can leave the hotel hands-free and stress-free, in grand fashion, not like a big, ol' sweaty pack mule.

HOW TO BE A GREAT HOST

If you want to be a great host, start with a phone call or e-mail to your guests to find out a few things that will help make their stay more relaxing, fun, and memorable. Make sure you know arrival and departure dates; double-check them by e-mail, text, or phone.

Here are some more tips that will help you be a wonderful host.

+ Ask your guests if they have food, pet, or down-feather allergies.

+ Share your agenda so your guests will know how to pack and what to prepare for. Is it going to be a fun, relaxing stay, a formal froufrou weekend, or a mixture?

+ Let your guests know about dinner plans, activities, sightseeing, and theater or concert tickets. Also inform them of obligations you may have, such as that from ten to one P.M. Saturday you have little Noah's soccer game, and they are welcome to join you or have some downtime or do some exploring. It's always a good idea to give your guests some breathing room.

+ Find out your guests' simple likes and dislikes. Are they tea or coffee drinkers, late sleepers or early risers? Once you have a few ideas of how to make your guests feel comfortable, you are off and running.

Here are some additional tips that will give your guests the things they need at their fingertips. If the host is relaxed, the guests will be relaxed, so the number-one gift you can offer your guests is to receive them in an open, calm, happy manner.

+ Show your guests where they will be sleeping and where the bathroom is. Then give them time to unpack and settle their things. Take them on a tour of the kitchen and pantry, and let them know they have an all-access pass to edibles and drinks.
+ If you have recreation areas such as a pool, sauna, billiard table, video games, etc., show your guests where they are and urge them to help themselves. Let them know your sleep and waking schedules so they will have an idea of the flow of your household. You could say something like "We are late sleepers, so the bagels, tea, coffee, etc., are in the kitchen by the stove. Feel free to help yourself in the morning." Also, "We usually go to bed around eleven P.M., but please feel free to go to bed earlier or anytime you like."

Below are a few things to have on hand to enhance your guests' stay.

+ Two types of pillows—soft and firm
+ A clock radio or iPod with stand, and a great mix of music with simple directions on how to use
+ Current magazines and a book or two on the nightstand
+ A house key, map, and directions to local attractions and such places as pharmacies and local stores
+ A basket with liquid body wash, shampoo, conditioner, hand lotion, mini-deodorant, Q-tips, cotton balls, water bottles, mini-chocolates, gum, Life Savers, wet wipes, and antibacterial hand soap
+ A box of tissues
+ Disposable razors
+ Toothbrush, toothpaste, and mini-mouthwash
+ Aspirin and antacids
+ A small calendar

HOW TO BE A GREAT HOUSEGUEST

Do you want to be remembered as a great houseguest? Be sure to call before you visit and ask your hosts important things such as what their soft schedule is and whether it will be a fancy, formal weekend or a sporty, flip-flop one. Ask how you might help with things, and find out about your hosts' children's and pets' schedules. Inquire about your hosts' sleep and wake-up times. If you have food, fragrance, or pet allergies, let your hosts know. Inform them of the times you will be arriving and departing, and the window of time you won't be available if you have something planned.

Following are more tips that will increase your chances of being invited back as a houseguest.

- **The three-day rule.** Remember that guests and fish truly stink after three days, so adhere to the three-day rule if possible. Your aim should be to accommodate your hosts' schedule and rhythm. Be an asset with your conversation, willingness to pitch in, being a fun part of what your hosts have planned, and knowing when they need a little breathing space. It's a fine and delicate balancing act, but easy to achieve if you remain alert and observant. The best way to add value is to be positive in your words and actions. Help change the subject if conversations or jokes start going in an inappropriate direction.
- When you arrive, make sure to stow all your belongings in one place; don't leave things scattered all over the house. Keep your toiletries in a waterproof bag, and don't leave them on the counter of the bathroom. Keep them with your other belongings. Make sure to make your bed whether it's in a private guest room or a foldout sofa bed. Wipe down the shower and the sink in the bathroom, and offer to help with the breakfast, lunch, and dinner prep, also with washing the dishes. Pitch in with other activities

such as shopping, vacuuming, taking out the trash, walking the dog.

- ✦ Always bring a gift. It could be a bestselling book your host would enjoy, a basket of seasonal fruit, several bottles of designer liquid hand soaps, unscented candles, a picture frame, two bottles of your favorite wine, or a new game. If your hosts have children and pets, it's a nice gesture to also bring small gifts for them, too.
- ✦ Being a gracious guest is a must, so send a handwritten letter of thanks as soon as you return home safely from your stay. Make sure you take your time and be detailed and complimentary. Write the note on good-quality, attractive stationery. Don't be tempted to send your thanks via e-mail.

ADDITIONAL HOUSEGUEST TIPS

- ✦ Arrive and depart on schedule.
- ✦ Treat your hosts' other guests, friends, neighbors, children, pets, and personal space with respect.
- ✦ If personal things are in plain view, such as packets of pictures, business and personal papers, opened laptop screens, don't leaf through them or sneak a peek. Give a wide range if your host is on the phone; no listening in.
- ✦ Keep your voice, TV, handhelds, Skyping, YouTube surfing, and computer at a low volume in the early-morning hours and late at night.
- ✦ If you accidentally break something (hopefully not the urn with Uncle Fred's ashes), tell your host. Don't make a big deal out of it, just apologize and replace the item as soon as possible.
- ✦ Be adaptable. If your host suggests a tennis match, don't yammer on about your tennis elbow and how you can't play. Instead, offer to keep score, serve water, or retrieve orphaned tennis balls.
- ✦ Know how to entertain yourself. Bring a book, an iPod,

walking shoes, knitting, or take that much-needed nap or catch up with friends via social media.

+ Offer to take your hosts to dinner, cook them dinner, treat them to a movie or a sporting event.

+ Don't be a water hog by taking lengthy baths and showers, especially if there are multiple guests and/or family members.

+ When it's time to leave, gather all of your belongings and replace or replenish anything that you've borrowed (except for toiletries provided by the host). Strip the bed linens, put the bedspread or duvet back on the bed, fold the dirty linens and pillowcases, and place them at the foot of the bed.

+ Don't tag the entire weekend on Facebook or tweet it out without asking the hosts and others present for the weekend stay if it's okay. Some people don't care to have their entire weekend launched into cyberspace for the whole universe to see.

PACKING FOR A TRIP

+ Have children pack their toys, coloring books, and music to keep them entertained, in their own backpacks.

+ Earplugs are important. Although we know your children will be on their best behavior, we can't control others around us, so earplugs will save you from the craziness. They will also help if you or your child is bothered by air-pressure changes in an airplane.

+ Your carry-on bag is your essentials bag. Be sure to pack it with items you may need if your luggage is lost, such as a compartmentalized bag for your digital camera, extra battery, cords, smartphone charger, and your iPod as well.

+ Use plastic storage bags to pack your small, loose essentials, such as jewelry.

+ Use a sassy passport organizer not only for your passport, but also your important papers and money to tip the flight attendant for snacks.

+ Don't forget to pack your medicines and toiletries in your

HAVE CHILDREN PACK THEIR TOYS, COLORING BOOKS, AND MUSIC TO KEEP THEM ENTERTAINED, IN THEIR OWN BACKPACKS.

ROLL YOUR GARMENTS TO SAVE SPACE, AND ROLL THEM IN TISSUE PAPER TO REDUCE WRINKLES.

YOUR CARRY-ON BAG IS YOUR ESSENTIALS BAG. PACK ITEMS YOU MAY NEED IF YOUR LUGGAGE IS LOST.

USE PLASTIC STORAGE BAGS FOR SMALL LOOSE ITEMS, MEDICINES AND TOILETRIES.

carry-on bag. Place them in those wonderful plastic storage bags to keep them safe and to avoid spillage. Also, minimize the size of your toiletries to allow for more space.

+ Since many airlines don't offer many snacks, or if you have allergies, pack some vittles in your carry-on bag to avoid the munchies and grouchiness that accompanies hunger pangs.

+ Take along some books or magazines to make your flight quick and entertaining.

+ Pack an extra pair of reading glasses.

+ When traveling, be sure to pack in two color schemes. This makes it much easier to pack and to mix-and-match outfits on your trip.

- Pack shoes in plastic storage bags to avoid spillage or tears from shoe heels.
- Roll your garments before putting them in your bag. This somehow allows for more space. If you roll them with tissue paper, they will be less wrinkled.

TRAVELING BY TRAIN

The following guidelines will help make you a considerate train traveler.

- Walk with the crowd and not through it as you head for the train. While searching for a seat, yield to the elderly, those with infants, disabled people with guide dogs, and expectant mothers.
- Once you get settled in your seat, remember you aren't at the beach, so no spreading out over two or three seats with your magazines, music, and snacks. Keep to your seat and space; don't be a space invader.
- Keep all odors to a minimum, such as from your feet, fragrance, and pungent foods. Please (please!) keep your shoes on until you are in the comfort of your own home, and save the perfume for outdoor events.
- Control your noise level. Refrain from loud, lengthy conversations on your cell phone; other travelers don't care about your breakup or Uncle Tom's goiter. While enjoying your music, make sure it's not offensive, especially to children, and be mindful of the amplification even if you're sporting earbuds. When talking to other travelers, make sure your volume is low and don't use foul language.
- Show respect to all people traveling with you. When the conductor comes by to take your ticket, have it out and ready. He doesn't want to stand there as your riffle through your backpack, briefcase, or big ol' purse. If an elderly or disabled person doesn't have a seat, give them yours! It will impress some and astonish many.

EVERYDAY ETIQUETTE

+ Please take your trash with you. This will help to keep the train clean for the travelers who come after you. Take your candy wrappers, newspapers, and anything else that wasn't there when you found your seat. While you're at it, why not go out on a limb and pick up any orphaned trash you see and dispose of it?

+ Anything that is better suited for the privacy of your own home, such as stretching out for a nap, snoring like a freight train, or public displays of affection, is best saved for after your train ride.

+ When you arrive at your destination, passing and walking through people is rude. Show respect by being patient and walking off with the crowd. If you have a big, bulky backpack, be mindful that smacking travelers in the face as you scurry by wasn't included in the price of the train ticket.

Nine

GIVING AND RECEIVING GIFTS

Regifting and What Getting Caught Taught Me

Every year my best friend, Wendi, has a Christmas cookie party for all the moms and kids in the neighborhood. Several years ago one of our friends, Shar, gave me a gift during the party. I didn't have a gift for her, so I went to Wendi and asked if she had anything I could give to Shar. Wendi said, "I have an ornament in my regift box that we can give to her." So we looked over the beautiful ornament, tucked into a burgundy velvet pouch, attached a shiny new tag, and presented it to Shar.

As I gave it to her, I felt nervous and told a little fairy tale to try to add a personal touch: "When I saw this ornament in the store, it made me think of you." Shar was so appreciative of the gift and the sentiment. I felt great and congratulated myself on gracefully salvaging an awkward situation.

The party soon wound down and guests, including Shar, began leaving. We exchanged hugs as she took the gift and her kids and headed home down the block.

A few minutes later the phone rang. Shar was hysterically laughing on the other end. When she got home, she showed her husband the ornament, and inside the little burgundy velvet pouch she found a tiny gift tag that read *TO WENDI, LOVE FRANCINE*. As Wendi and I stood there in shock, Shar said she was just so happy that she had busted the etiquette coach for regifting!

So, take it from me, if you regift, make sure all the tags are off and the gift is put in brand-new packaging. The upside of this story is that we have created a new tradition by trading the ornament back and forth each Christmas at the cookie party with the statement "When I saw this ornament in the store, it made me think of you."

In giving and receiving gifts, the thought is what counts. People want to know that you care, that you spent a little time on them, and that you put some thought into selecting the gift. It's not necessary to spend a lot of money, especially if you don't have it to spend. If someone is more focused on how much you spent than on the sentiment behind the gift, that's their problem, not yours.

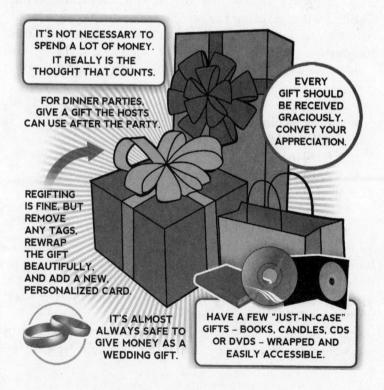

IT'S NOT NECESSARY TO SPEND A LOT OF MONEY. IT REALLY IS THE THOUGHT THAT COUNTS.

FOR DINNER PARTIES, GIVE A GIFT THE HOSTS CAN USE AFTER THE PARTY.

EVERY GIFT SHOULD BE RECEIVED GRACIOUSLY. CONVEY YOUR APPRECIATION.

REGIFTING IS FINE, BUT REMOVE ANY TAGS, REWRAP THE GIFT BEAUTIFULLY, AND ADD A NEW, PERSONALIZED CARD.

IT'S ALMOST ALWAYS SAFE TO GIVE MONEY AS A WEDDING GIFT.

HAVE A FEW "JUST-IN-CASE" GIFTS – BOOKS, CANDLES, CDS OR DVDS – WRAPPED AND EASILY ACCESSIBLE.

As a gift recipient, the most important thing is to convey your appreciation for the other person's time, effort, and expense. Remember, not everyone has the financial ability to purchase expensive gifts, and every gift should be received graciously.

GIFT GIVING

Dinner Parties

While it's a good idea to bring a small gift to a dinner party, be careful about bringing flowers or wine. The hosts have probably selected particular flowers to display and particular wines to serve with the meal. They may not have a vase available for your flowers, and they may not want to serve your wine that evening. If you do bring wine, make sure to tell the hosts that it's for them to enjoy later, and that they don't have to pair it with anything that evening.

Here are some good choices for dinner-party gifts.

+ Champagne
+ Unscented candles
+ A little book of quotes
+ A CD
+ A small decorative item for the home, such as a letter opener or paperweight

Just-in-Case Gifts

It can be awkward to receive a holiday gift when you don't have something to offer in return, but there's a simple solution. Have a few gifts wrapped up and easily accessible so that you never have to say, "But I didn't get you anything!"

Make sure these just-in-case gifts are appropriate for both men and women, and keep some children's gifts handy as well. If you purchase these gifts in advance, you can take advantage of sales and stock up so you don't have to shop at the last minute.

Here are some good just-in-case gift ideas.

- ✦ For adults: music, books, candles, DVDs, and gift cards.
- ✦ For kids: iTunes cards and books are a safe bet. You can usually find great deals on children's books if you buy them in advance of the holidays.

No Gifts

When an invitation says "no gifts," you should respect that request.

- ✦ You can give a wonderful card with a special message instead.
- ✦ If you really feel that a card isn't enough, consider making a donation to the host's favorite charity.

People may request "no gifts" for many reasons. Perhaps they don't have room in their home for more things, or they don't want guests to feel obligated to spend money. Whatever the reason, it's the hosts' decision and should be respected.

Perfect Personal Gift Ideas

When choosing the perfect gift for loved ones, make sure it is personal and specific to their interests, desires, and passions.

- ✦ A homemade CD with all the songs that remind you of your loved one.
- ✦ Frame the lyrics to your wedding song and have it delivered to their office.
- ✦ If your loved one enjoys dancing, singing, painting, cooking, etc., you can buy them a series of classes to indulge in their secret passion.

+ Make a contribution to their favorite charity and offer to spend the day with them volunteering.
+ Buy a bibliophile a first edition of a favorite book. If it's signed, even better.
+ Detail their car, dislodging the french fries that have been in the carpet since the new millennium.
+ If their love language is food and dining out is their thing, make a reservation, secure a babysitter, and dazzle them with your impeccable dining skills.

Selecting Gifts

Think carefully about your intended recipient when selecting a gift. Do they like to read? Will they have time to use that gift certificate to the spa? What are the recipients' hobbies or favorite activities? Have they commented favorably on an item that's within your budget? If necessary, get help from someone who knows the recipient better than you do.

The closer your relationship to the person, the more carefully you should think about the gift to ensure that it's something they would enjoy. Giving a tin of cookies to a friend who's on a sugar-free diet is almost worse than giving nothing at all. It shows that you haven't been paying attention to what's going on in your friend's life.

If you're having trouble coming up with a creative gift idea, try combining a few related items in a gift basket or gift bag. Here are some possibilities to get you started.

+ For a friend who loves to cook—an apron, an Italian cookbook, and a bottle of extra-virgin olive oil.
+ For someone who loves to read—a book light, a beautiful bookmark, and a gift card to a bookstore.
+ For a new mom—comfy slippers, a light robe, and a few of her favorite snacks (sometimes it's hard for new moms to get to the store).

- For a sports fan—tickets to a game, a team T-shirt or cap, and a mug with a team logo.
- For a golfer—a few tees, a package of golf balls, a golfing towel, and a golf umbrella.
- For a get-well gift—a book of crossword puzzles, a bed tray, and a collection of herbal teas. Or you can give a favorite book that seemed to make time fly when you read it.

Whatever gift you choose, make sure to include a card with a handwritten message from you. People tend to glance over the printed portion of the card, but will always read the handwritten note at the bottom.

Weddings

It's almost always safe to give money as a wedding gift, especially given the cost of weddings these days! Here are a few other options.

- Simply select something off the couple's wedding registry (if they have one). They really do want what they registered for.
- If you can't afford to give something big, just give what you can.
- Put their wedding invitation in a beautiful frame, write them a poem, or give them a handmade gift.

Whatever you do, don't skip the wedding because you're unable to give a splashy gift. Weddings are celebrations, and the most important thing is to share the experience with the happy couple.

RECEIVING GIFTS

The biggest question I get about receiving gifts is whether to open the gift immediately. The answer is that it depends on the situation.

Here are some ways to receive gifts smoothly.

+ When you're the guest of honor at an event where opening gifts is part of the entertainment (such as a baby shower), you should absolutely open gifts during the celebration.
+ Express appreciation for every gift, even the ones you're not crazy about, and never look or sound disappointed.
+ If you receive duplicate gifts (such as two coffeepots), reassure the gift givers by saying something like "I'm so glad, I can use one for regular and one for decaf!" or "It will be great to have a backup."
+ When opening gifts at an event, make sure to keep track of who gave you each gift so you can write thank-you notes later. Ask a friend or family member to help with this task so it doesn't slow things down too much. Keep a steady pace when opening gifts so the guests don't grow weary.
+ At other types of events (such as anniversary parties), some guests will bring gifts and others won't. In that case, put any gifts you receive to the side so that those who didn't bring gifts won't feel awkward.
+ Of course, if someone really wants you to open their gift right away, go ahead and open it. For many people, part of the fun of giving gifts is to see the recipient's reaction.
+ As soon as a gift is presented to you, make sure the person who gave the gift feels that you appreciate seeing them and receiving their gift.
+ Be sure to send each person away with the feeling that you were thrilled with their gift and appreciate the time and thought they put into selecting it. Being appreciated makes the person who gave the gift feel that their time and money were well spent.

REGIFTING

Etiquette experts disagree on the propriety of regifting (giving a gift that you received to someone else as a gift). There's no reason a gift should be discarded or go unused if you know a person who would like it. I believe that regifting is perfectly fine, as long as you follow a few basic rules.

+ Always rewrap the gift beautifully and add a new card. Make sure to remove anything (tags, cards, etc.) that indicates you received the item as a gift yourself.
+ Never regift in the same social circle. If you received the gift from a coworker, regift to someone you don't work with and who doesn't know the original gift giver.
+ Don't regift anything that looks even remotely used. Only brand-new items in the original packaging should be regifted.
+ Make sure the gift is something you think the recipient will like. Even though it's a regift, it's still a gift, which means you should put some thought into it and consider the recipient's likes and dislikes.

Ten

INVITATIONS, SYMPATHY CARDS, AND THANK-YOU NOTES

The Mighty Power of the Thank-You Note

The power of a thank-you note is more *vital* than most of us realize. Thank-you notes are so important because they hit all the senses. You see them, you hold them and feel them, and when you read them, it's emotional.

A friend who is the head of human resources and hiring for her company shared with me over dinner one night that she had tirelessly been working on narrowing down two hundred candidates for a top position in her company and had it down to two people at last. She had spent most of the day interviewing these two people, one of them over lunch.

She had to decide by the next day and was feeling a lot of angst. Both finalists were highly qualified and had wonderful social skills, references, and experience. We talked about the two candidates, and I could see why she was having a difficult time deciding.

She called me at eleven o'clock the next morning and told me she had made her choice. When I asked how she'd finally decided, she said she had gotten a note from one of the candidates thanking her for the lunch. It amazed her that it had arrived less than twenty-four hours after the lunch.

Thank-you notes are a golden key to unlocking major opportunities. Unfortunately, most people rarely use this key to the doors they long to open.

In another example, some years ago a young comedian's audition tape was rejected for a potential veejay spot on MTV. Although disappointed, she sent the producer a thank-you note for considering her for this coveted on-air job. The producer was so impressed by the gesture that he recommended her to sister network VH1, where she landed one of the veejay jobs. Rosie O'Donnell says, "A thank-you note got me that job."

EVITES / INVITATIONS / RSVP ETIQUETTE

Evites

Evite is a free social-planning Web site where you can create an online invitation, send it directly to your guests' e-mail addresses, then manage the guest list, all from your computer. An Evite is not as formal as a mailed invitation, but it is an efficient and easy way to keep track of who will be attending your social event. It is also economical and ecofriendly. Paperlesspost.com and Pingg.com are other choices for sending invitations via the World Wide Web.

Because an Evite appears less formal, people sometimes wonder if they have to respond. Of course you do. Put yourself in the host's shoes. They need an accurate count of who will be attending so they can provide enough space, food, and drinks. No host wants to check their guest list and see names in the "not yet replied" section.

Consider the following tips if you receive an Evite.

+ The host can see the date you viewed the invitation, so don't make them wait. Check your schedule and then take two seconds to reply. It is polite to do this within the first day or two of receiving an Evite.
+ With any invitation, formal or casual, be sure to let your yes be yes. Don't cancel because something better came up. Occasionally something unforeseen does pose a problem that you just cannot avoid. If this happens, call the host immediately and explain the situation.
+ You don't have to leave a remark in the comment box, but

it is polite to do so. Always take the time to thank the host for inviting you, even if you are unable to attend.

✦ If your Evite doesn't include "and guest," then don't ask if you can bring a friend, and definitely don't show up with someone, unless you are interested in creating an awkward situation. If the Evite does say "and guest," then be sure to let the host know if you are bringing someone and share their name.

✦ If you are the host, when sending Evites to single friends, it is courteous to allow them to bring a guest, especially if they have to travel to attend.

Invitations and RSVP

Whether for a birthday, wedding, dinner party, or any other occasion, an invitation comes with obligations that require your attention. Follow the tips below and there's a good chance you will remain on the guest list for future events.

✦ If you have ever wondered what RSVP stands for, it is *répondez s'il vous plaît* (French), meaning "please reply." This little abbreviation has been used for many years, asking for a prompt response to an invitation. It is courteous to reply within the first day or two of receiving the invitation.

✦ Be careful to reply in the method specified on the invitation. Some examples would be a handwritten note to the host, a response card, a phone call to the host, e-mail, regrets only, and no reply requested. If the invitation asks you to phone a response, don't send an e-mail or a handwritten note.

✦ Make sure you thank the host for sending you an invitation, even if you are unable to attend.

✦ Once you have responded that you will attend, you should not change your yes to a no. The few exceptions include illness, injury, the death of a relative or friend, or a business conflict you did not foresee and cannot get out of. If you must cancel, call your host right away. Never cancel because you received a better offer. It is always unacceptable to be a no-show. Changing a no to a yes is okay if it does not alter the host's plans.

+ Invitations are sent to the people the host wants to invite and no one else, so don't ask if you can bring anyone unless the invitation specifically notes "and guest." If allowed to invite a guest, specify that you are bringing someone and state the person's name when you reply.

SYMPATHY CARDS

It's not easy to find the right words when someone you know loses a loved one, but it's important to try. Here are a few tips for writing condolence notes, followed by a couple of samples to get you started.

+ Send the note as soon as possible after hearing the news.
+ Use stationery or a blank greeting card, and write a message in either blue or black ink.
+ Express your sympathy. It can be as simple as "I am so sorry for your loss."
+ If you're having trouble finding the right words, say so: "It's so hard to find the right words at a time like this."
+ If you knew the deceased, add a personal memory: "I used to play cards with your mother every Sunday and thoroughly enjoyed her company. When I was down, she always knew just what to say to make me feel better."
+ If you're close to the person to whom you are writing and you genuinely want to help, offer to do so. But be specific. Saying "Let me know what I can do to help" is unlikely to elicit a response and puts the burden on the bereaved to think of something for you to do or to respond to you. A more meaningful offer would be "If it's all right with you, I'd like to come over and make dinner for you and your family or drop off dinner next Wednesday or Friday. I'll give you a call to find out what night would be best."

✦ End the note with a few comforting words, such as "You are in my thoughts and prayers."

Sample Sympathy Cards

Dear Estelle,

I was so sad to hear about the death of your husband. He was a wonderful man—kind, giving, funny, and generous. He will truly be missed.

It's so hard to find the right words at a time like this, but I want you to know that you're in my thoughts.

With deepest sympathy,
Geraldine

Dear Susan,

I am so sorry for your loss. Your father was such a special person, and I know how close the two of you were. I only wish I had some way to ease your pain.

Next week, after your mother goes back to Florida, I would like to bring you dinner. I'll give you a call to find out what night works best for you.

You are in my thoughts,
Anita

THANK-YOU NOTES

It is appropriate to send a thank-you note when you receive a gift, the sooner the better. When it comes to weddings and baby showers, you have a little grace period. You have up to three months to send thank-you notes for wedding gifts, and two months for baby-shower gifts, but it's still smart to send them sooner, if possible. The old etiquette rule about having up to a year to send thank-you notes for wedding gifts is no longer acceptable. And remember, the quicker you send your note, the less elaborate it has to be.

It is a good idea to send thank-you notes following these occasions as well:

- ✦ When someone does you a favor
- ✦ When people have been particularly hospitable (such as hosting you in their home for the night)
- ✦ Parties and dinners hosted by others
- ✦ Special acts of kindness
- ✦ Good service
- ✦ Volunteering and helpfulness
- ✦ An interview (job, college)

How to Write a Thank-You Note

Don't get bogged down trying to find the perfect stationery or the perfect words to express your gratitude. The important thing is to get a short note written and out the door as soon as possible.

Here are a few things to remember when writing a thank-you note.

- ✦ It doesn't need to be long or a dissertation.
- ✦ Address the note to whoever signed the card that accompanied the gift.
- ✦ Mention the gift and be specific. Avoid general statements such as "Thank you for the lovely gift." If the gift was a cashmere sweater, say, "Thank you for the lovely cashmere sweater."
- ✦ Describe how you're going to use the gift if possible ("This sweater will be perfect for the ski trip we're taking next month!").
- ✦ Recognize any special thought or care that went into the gift ("It was so kind of you to remember how much I love cashmere and that blue is my favorite color").
- ✦ Include a sentence or two about your life ("We are so looking forward to the ski trip. We haven't taken a vacation in ages! It will be great to get away").
- ✦ Sign the note ("All the best, Karen"). You can also use "Love," "With thanks," "Sincerely," or any other closing that you feel comfortable with.
- ✦ Thank-you notes should be handwritten and sent by regular mail (not e-mail). If you have messy handwriting, just write slowly and do your best to make it legible.
- ✦ Be yourself. You don't have to use any fancy language or words that you would never use in real life.

Sample Thank-You Notes

Dear Aunt Joy,

I just received the book light you sent for my birthday. What a perfect gift! Now I can read in bed without disturbing Bobby. I'll think of you every time I use it. Hope you and the kids are doing well.

Love,
Angelina

Dear Kelly Ann,

It was so kind of you and Dom to open your home to us last weekend. We really enjoyed our trip to Seattle and can't thank you enough for your hospitality.

If you're ever in Boston, we hope you'll stay with us, although we can't guarantee that our French toast will be as delicious as yours!

Best wishes,
Kristin & Steve Cronin

Dear Aunt Liz,

Thank you so much for the beautiful silk scarf. I just love the colors and the pattern you chose. In fact, I like it so much I'm planning to wear it to my college interview tomorrow! I'll let you know how it goes. Thanks again for thinking of me.

All the best,
Jennifer

Dear Yvonne & Tom,

We just received the adorable baby clothes you sent and can't wait to put them on Ava. I especially love the pink outfit with the matching hat and socks!

Ava is doing great since we brought her home, and Jackson seems to like being an older brother so far. We look forward to seeing you at the baby naming next month.

Love,
Michelle & Robby Fleishman

Dear Maria & Harrison,

Thank you so much for bringing us dinner last week! With a newborn at home it's not easy to get out to the store or a restaurant, so we really appreciated the homemade meal. How did you know that Italian food is our favorite?

We feel truly fortunate to have such wonderful friends and hope to see you again soon.

Warmly,
Dee, Pepper, and Jason

Sample of a Formal Thank-You Letter After an Interview

Your Name
Address
City, State, Zip Code
Phone Number
E-mail
Date

Interviewer's Name
Title
Organization
Address
City, State, Zip Code

Dear Mr. Pucci:

Thank you for taking the time out of your busy schedule to speak with me about the Social Media Publicist position with Branding Specialist Corporation.

After speaking with you, I believe that I am a perfect candidate for the position. I possess the ability to adapt and learn quickly and in my eagerness to perform well would bring the technical and analytical skills necessary to get the job done.

Please feel free to contact me at any time if further information is needed. My cell phone number is (123) 456-7890. I am very interested in working for you and look forward to hearing from you once the final decision is made regarding this position.

Again, thank you for your time and consideration.

Sincerely,
Andrea Miller

Eleven

OUT AND ABOUT

Common Sense Will Get You Everywhere

One day my dad called me. We spoke for a minute, then I let him know I had to go since my trainer was waiting to run with me. My dad responded, "Patricia, you knew how to run since you were about twelve months old. Are you really paying this trainer?" I laughed as we hung up and thought my dad had a great point.

Dad called me back later in the week, asking how my day was and what we were up to for the weekend. I told him my husband and I had been invited to go fishing with a client in Boca Grande, Florida, who had hired a fishing guide. I heard nothing but crickets on the other end of the phone. "Daddy, are you there?" I asked. I thought we had been disconnected. He said, "What exactly does this guide do?" I said, "Well, they drive the boat to the best fishing spot, they bait your hook, then they cast your line." Crickets again, then he said, "Patricia, you've been fishing since you were two. Seems like that guide is getting to have all the fun and you are all paying him." As my dad said good-bye, I heard him mumbling, "Just doesn't make any sense."

A third call came from my dad the following week: "What are y'all up to?" I said, "The boys are going to farm camp on Monday." My dad said, "Farm camp? What do they do at this farm camp?" I said, "Oh, it's wonderful. They bale hay, clean out stalls, feed all the livestock, they even get to milk a real cow." My dad said, excited, "That's the best news. It will teach the boys the value of hard work and that they get paid for it, too." Before I could think, I said, "Oh, no, Daddy, we pay for the boys to go." Crickets again. Then my dad (who hates flying) said, "I've got to get a flight to Florida right away. You were smart when we sent you to college in Florida, and now it seems like you've lost all your common sense."

ART MUSEUMS

Museums are places to fill our visual and emotional senses. They offer treasures from faraway places and take us on journeys that we couldn't go on any other way. Art means so many different things to so many different people. Remember that museums aren't just for the froufrou, chichi, or la-di-da; they are for all of us.

Here are some tips to make your next trip to the museum memorable.

- ✦ Leave that big ol' bulky backpack or oversize pocketbook in the trunk of your car. If you are uncomfortable leaving them behind, call ahead to see if the museum has a coat or bag check. It's difficult to have a good time if you knock over a vase from the Ming Dynasty.
- ✦ Take advantage of the docent, which is just a fancy name for a tour guide. Docents take people in groups, or one-on-one, and explain the art and where it came from so visitors can have a deeper understanding and appreciation.
- ✦ Remember the three-foot rule, where you stand at least three feet away from whomever you're speaking to? Well, the same goes for artwork. Only touch with your eyes.
- ✦ Cameras and cell phone cameras are not allowed because the flash photography can damage the artwork.
- ✦ No food or drinks are allowed in the exhibit areas; dispose of them before entering the museum.
- ✦ If you are going to sketch, draw, or take notes, be sure to use a pencil. Never, ever use ink of any color to sketch, as it isn't allowed in most museums. Stray ink can cause irreversible damage to the artwork.

NO CAMERAS OR CELL PHONE CAMERAS.

STAND BACK AT LEAST 3 FEET.

NO BULKY BAGS.

✦ Talk quietly so you do not disturb other visitors, and be sure to follow all posted museum rules.

BEACH DAY

As the weather, surf, and sand beckon us to its beaches, all generations, from toddlers to teens, new parents, and retirees, respond to the invitation for fun, sun, and relaxation.

Here are a few tips to insure a collectively magical day at the beach.

- When scouting out your perfect patch of tranquillity, remember to keep a distance of at least five feet from your fellow sunbathers.
- Chances are, the tide will come up while you are at the beach, so don't park your personal effects too close to the water. You won't want to have to move all your stuff later and possibly crowd others.
- When your feet hit the sand, remove your flip-flops, as this fashionable beachwear has the uncanny ability to flick sand everywhere.
- Keep your music low and the content appropriate. Refrain from singing along loudly to your amped-up iPod.
- Keep a considerable distance from others if you are smoking or having a loud, lengthy conversation on your cell phone.
- Never, ever feed the seagulls, as they may leave an unwelcome deposit on you or the people near you. Beach-dwelling birds have also been known to pilfer food from unsuspecting visitors, so keep yours covered.
- Be mindful of other people when shaking sand off your towel and be aware of which way the wind is blowing, as nobody came to the beach for a free microdermabrasion.
- Refrain from foul language and inappropriate conversation. Consideration is the key in all social situations.
- Remember to recycle. Bring plastic bags to hold all your recyclables and trash, just in case a trash can is not available.
- It's important to protect the environment by respecting sand dunes, turtle nests, sea creatures, and plant life.
- Avoid overt public displays of affection. Be conscious of those around you and keep expressions of adoration private.

BOATING

There is only one captain, so all eyes and ears must be turned in their direction and follow their lead. The captain's main goal is to keep passengers and fellow boaters from danger, while insuring that a fun and relaxing day is shared by all. So heed the rules, regulations, and prompts from your captain, as well as the tips below.

+ The number-one rule of boating is safety first.
+ Most accidents happen while people are boarding the boat. That is why it's important to wear nonskid shoes to prevent slipping and falling. Never, ever steady yourself on the windshield, the poles, or the antennae of a boat. Always hold on to a solid and sturdy part of the boat while getting on.
+ If you have heavy cargo, such as an ice chest or a big ol' beach bag, go ahead and put that on the dock, board the boat, and then bring your goods on board. Be respectful of the limited space on the boat and do not overpack. Make sure your belongings are secure and not susceptible to sliding around.
+ If in doubt, ask the captain where to get on, where to sit, and how you can be of help.
+ The life vest is necessary for your safety, so go ahead and wear it.
+ If you have been lucky enough to be invited onto a boat for the day, go into your wallet and get out some of your dead presidents to give to your host to cover the cost of gas. Another wonderful gesture would be to offer to bring the food and beverages for the day.
+ At the end of the day, ask the captain if you can help put the boat away. Make sure all the end-of-trip chores are finished before leaving. Every captain has developed a system that keeps things running smoothly, and your offer of help will certainly be appreciated.

EVERYDAY ETIQUETTE

CONCERTS

If you have a favorite artist you would love to see in person, start out by going to their Web site to find out about their upcoming events and shows. Also check newspapers, magazines, Twitter, and Facebook for any recent news and happenings.

Here are more tips to follow when in the presence of your favorite performer.

- Purchase tickets as soon as you know you want to go to their show. Don't waste time because you may lose the opportunity if the tickets sell out quickly.
- Always show respect for opening acts. Remember they may just become the next big thing. We know you paid to see the main act, but relax, enjoy, and encourage the opening performers with applause and attention.
- Set changes last about twenty to thirty-five minutes. They are arduous and tedious for the crew and the band, so no yelling at the soundboard technicians or stagehands changing the set. Use this time to stretch your legs, get a drink or something to eat, and visit the restroom.
- Do not shout out a request unless you are 100 percent sure the artist sings it and that the song hasn't already been sung. If a ballad is being performed, never yell, "I love you." That is just annoying. Keep your screaming to a minimum and no whistling, as anything loud enough for the band to hear may hurt another fan's ears. Refrain from singing so loudly that the people around you can't hear the singer.
- At the end of the show, you may want to visit the artist's merchandise tables to buy some products. At most venues the tables will be at the entrances and exits. Possibly you would like to linger out by the tour bus in hopes of getting an autograph when the artist leaves. Perhaps you will want to stay inside by the stage, hoping a roadie will throw you some guitar picks or maybe a drumstick. Better

yet, you might get an invitation to go backstage and meet the artist.

+ The days of flicking your Bic are almost gone, due to the new fire codes, unless you're at an outdoor show. These days most fans simply hold up their cell phones or special cell phone applications depicting a lighter.

BACKSTAGE MEET-AND-GREET

+ Never give an artist a framed picture of the both of you from a concert ten years ago, as they have many fans and limited space on their bus. Keep the memento for yourself, and treasure the past experience.

+ Be sure to stand up when you meet the entertainer. The artist has just performed an amazing show while you've had a handy seat nearby, so stand to greet them, and remain standing until the meet-and-greet has concluded.

+ If you are seeking an autograph, have your Sharpie ready to use, cap off.

+ If you bring albums or other artist memorabilia to be signed, be aware that the artist reserves the right to sign what they choose. So always carry a ticket stub or program in the event they refuse to sign that cherished album from your youth.

+ Be sure you know the artist and their music. Don't ask why they didn't sing your favorite song, only to find out it isn't one of their hits or they never recorded it.

+ Do not launch into a dissertation about how you met twelve years ago at a Red Rock concert and ask if they remember you, as other people are waiting to speak with the artist. Spend one to three minutes with the performer, then move aside and let other people have a chance to meet and greet.

+ Don't plunder the food and drinks backstage, as it is usually reserved for the entertainers and their crew.

+ Be sure to stand at least three feet away from whomever you are speaking with. If you find that the person you are talking to keeps backing away, it probably means you are standing too close.

THINGS YOU SHOULD SAY
DURING A MEET-AND-GREET

+ Show appreciation for the artist's songs, especially the obscure ones; this sets you apart as a loyal fan.
+ Always start with a compliment—saying how much you loved the show. Ask how they liked playing in the particular theater or venue.
+ Say you appreciate them coming to your town and that you've waited many years for them to come, or you took off work to stand in line for a ticket or to be the first logged in to purchase online.
+ "Tonight's show was just amazing! What song did you enjoy performing the most?"
+ "How do you stay in such great shape? How do you perform for two hours straight without getting winded? You make it look effortless."
+ "You sounded great—just like you did ten or twenty years ago. Do you do vocal exercises to get yourself ready before the show?"
+ "What is the best and worst thing about touring?"
+ "Who was your musical mentor or inspiration?"

THINGS YOU SHOULD NOT SAY
DURING A MEET-AND-GREET

+ "Wow! You look skinny in person."
+ "You remind me of Elvis, only he had hair."
+ "Did you have a cold tonight? You sound different on your CD."
+ "Do you really play that piano or is it just a prop?"
+ "I know your aunt's former second-grade student who now cuts my uncle Neil's hair. Can I be in your band?"
+ "I don't care for rock music; I just came because my sister dragged me here. Will you sign my ticket?"

- "Did you pick out that outfit?"
- "When I stopped smoking, I gained thirty pounds, too."
- "You sounded pretty good, but nothing like Elton John—he's my favorite."
- "Can you let me see what a tour bus looks like if I promise not to touch anything?"
- "Can I have a free ticket to your next show?"

DATING DOS AND DON'TS

Dating is a wonderful way to make new friends, learn new things, and maybe discover a life partner. It can also lead to a business connection or a date for another friend. The best way to navigate a date is to start with kindness and respect.

Here are some dos and don'ts when it comes to dating.

DOS

- Be on time so your date is not kept waiting. Being punctual speaks volumes about your character and gets the date off to a good start.
- A first date is a delicate balance of listening and asking questions. Ask questions and repeat the answers to your date so they will feel heard and valued. Just be careful that your date doesn't feel as if it's an interrogation or investigation. Keep it light and fun. Try to keep the conversation balanced with both parties asking and answering questions.
- The person who does the inviting does the paying. It is always nice to offer to pay half, and definitely pick up the bill on the second date if you didn't pay on the first one.
- Always be gracious and thankful for the time shared, knowing your date intended to show you a pleasurable time. Mention each thing you did together—the dinner, movie, laughter, and drinks—and say, "Thank you."

DON'TS

- ✦ Don't overshare personal information about your life and/or family. It isn't the time to bring all the family skeletons out of the closet or to get all your lifetime blunders out in the open. We've all lived our lives and made choices that weren't always the best, but the first date isn't the time to bare your soul.
- ✦ Don't brag about your money, job, car, or calf implants. It's unflattering and leaves a person wondering what in the world you're hiding. People will learn about your good qualities and assets in due time. Don't show your entire hand on the fist date.
- ✦ Don't ever speak in a derogatory manner to a server or the waitstaff. This includes snapping your fingers and firing "Hey, you" across the room. It doesn't impress your date and leaves a negative impression with your date and the restaurant staff.
- ✦ Never lie, smoke, or try to be overly funny with your date.
- ✦ Don't dig up bones from the past; leave them buried. Your date doesn't want to hear about your past relationship and how she stole your dog and best hunting gun in the middle of the night.
- ✦ Don't promise to call if you have no intention of calling. You will surely run into that person again and it will be awkward.

Blind Date

Blind dating can be a blast, unless the focus is on the person being the one, the one true love. That is a lot to expect from a first date. So go with the goal to laugh, make a new friend, and have fun. It's best to meet for coffee, drinks, or dessert because that whole five-course-meal thing makes the stakes too high.

- ✦ Beware, no talking about past relationships!
- ✦ First dates are a time of new beginnings, so focus on what's in front of you and not what's behind you.

- Refrain from talking about anything that's too personal, like "I was down in my bowels all week" or "Did you hear about my bout with gout?" A better topic might be who most inspires you and how they have affected your life, or your most prized possession, or a favorite trip or hobby.
- Blind dates can be awkward, so always give them a second try. Besides, first-date stories always make great wedding-toast material!

Online Dating

Online dating offers a comfortable way to meet people while hunkered down behind your computer in the safe confines of your home. Here are a few guidelines to insure safety before venturing out on a date with someone you've met online.

- Always be honest in your online description and photo. Lies will eventually be found out, so start the right way with a truthful picture and bio.
- If you find someone of interest, let the online chat scoot on over to a cell phone chat. You can learn much more about a person from the way they speak and carry on a conversation in real time.
- Google the person if possible; it's always best to be safe rather than sorry.
- Don't disclose personal information unless you are highly comfortable and ready for the next level of communicating. A well-intentioned person would never push you to share such things. Your place of work, home address, home phone number, and e-mail should be kept private.
- If you do take it beyond the cell phone chat, let it be in a coffee shop, and preset the duration of the meeting, saying, "I can meet from two to three P.M., then I am meeting my sister for dinner." Also, let two people know where you are meeting and all the data from the Internet you have on this person, just to be on the safe side.

FRAGRANCE IN PUBLIC

Perfume can be applied in many ways, but we only need to remember two words: *subtle* and *discreet*. Your perfume should never shout, it should whisper.

When purchasing a fragrance, invest in quality, as the cheaper aromas are often offensive and do not enhance your persona.

Here are a few tips in boosting your essence.

✦ There are some places where we should never wear perfume. The top three are hospitals, airplanes, and job interviews.

✦ Use every ounce of discretion when wearing fragrance to the theater, church, or anywhere else you are in proximity to other people. Wearing perfume in the workplace isn't a great idea either.

✦ Applying an elegant scent is a personal matter, just like putting on your undergarments. It should always be applied in private, never in public.

✦ Perfume can be overpowering and can sometimes cause nausea, migraines, asthma, and even anaphylaxis.

✦ Aftershave can have an overpowering scent as well, so use it sparingly.

✦ Applying fragrance to your clothing or sensitive parts of your skin can have unpleasant results.

✦ Gold, silver, and stone are not affected by perfume, but beware, it can dull the surface of your pearls!

✦ Light and heat are the biggest enemies of the longevity and quality of fragrance, so store it in the crisper drawer of your refrigerator in a ziplock bag where it is cool and dark. I know it sounds crazy, but carrots are about a dollar an ounce and perfume can be up to one hundred an ounce.

✦ If people are tearing, wheezing, sneezing, and backing away from you slowly, you may have been overzealous in your spritzing, so lighten up some.

✦ Remember, sometimes less is more (appealing)!

GETTING AROUND

Yes, protocol governs getting around with ease and grace. Following are some tips to help you navigate various modes of transport.

- Let's start with elevators. I know, I know, it's just a little square box that goes up and down, but it makes people act crazy! If you approach an elevator and the button has already been pressed, please don't pretend you are on a game show and keep pressing it. If you are walking up to an elevator and the doors are closing, don't play survival of the fittest by trying to jam through the closing door. Just stand there calmly and wait because, I promise you, the elevator will come back. If you find yourself inside and you are not close to the number panel, please don't reach over men, women, children, and animals to get to the number. Just politely ask someone to press your number. If you find yourself positioned beside the number panel, calmly look around and say, "What number, please?"
- Next stop is the escalator. Keep to the right if you are standing still. If you prefer to pass, do so on the left, remembering to say "Excuse me" to the people you are passing. I don't know what happens to people in going from the top to the bottom, but they must have some kind of religious experience, because when they step off, they freeze! Perhaps they are pondering the meaning of life. But six tons of steel are coming at you with people on it; you've got to keep moving. Know the direction you are going to walk in when you step off the escalator. You have three choices—right, left, or straight. Just keep moving.
- That goes for revolving doors, too. Once that little circular door shoots you out, keep moving!
- When walking on sidewalks, stairs, escalators, with shopping carts in the grocery store, or in the mall, remember to keep to the right. If you stay to the right, you

will never go wrong. Different countries do have different policies. Check which side of the road to walk on before traveling. If the country's traffic drives on the left, people usually walk to the left, also.

+ Whichever side is the standard, pedestrian traffic should keep moving forward in a timely manner. If walking with a stroller or large suitcase, be mindful of where you are going. Keep talking and texting on a cell phone to a minimum, as you are taking up the space of three people.

+ If you see friends and decide to chat, move to an area of the walkway where you won't impede others.

+ Try your best to walk with the flow of traffic and not through it. If you have to stop suddenly, do your best to move to the side so people don't bump into one another in a chain reaction.

+ Don't form a chain gang walking side by side. Single file, or two by two, is best on busy sidewalks, and at malls and sporting events.

+ Never, ever spit while walking.

THE GROCERY STORE

Shopping at the grocery store may seem like a chore, but it can be quite relaxing and pleasurable if you go with the proper attitude. Even taking children with you can be good. It can be a learning experience for them and a time to build memories, preferably fond ones. Just keep the following common courtesies in mind.

+ Rescue orphaned grocery carts in the parking lot and roll them back to their proper resting place. Besides assuring yourself of a cart when you get into the store, you may prevent a runaway cart from T-boning an automobile, sparing someone a trip to the Dent Doctor.

+ Yield to the people exiting the store before you attempt to enter.

+ Don't be a middle-of-the-aisle blocker, stopping other

shoppers from passing on either side. Keep your cart to the right as you travel up and down each aisle.

+ The grocery store isn't a bedroom, so no wearing pajamas or house slippers.

+ If you accidentally cause a spill or spot one, report it so no one gets hurt.

+ If you don't want to be known as a "yell phone shopper," then show respect for the cashier by refraining from multitasking. Talk to the cashier and not on your cell phone when checking out.

+ When in the express lane, stick to the rules of ten items or less. You will appreciate the same respect the next time you are trying to check out in a hurry.

+ Payment procrastinators are the worst offenders in the supermarket checkout line. Don't wait until the last minute to fill out your check; start while groceries are being rung up so at the end all you need to write in is the total. Also make sure to have your credit or debit card out and ready to pay: no digging through purses or wallets once the total has been given.

+ Return unwanted items, especially perishables, to their rightful place or give them to the cashier.

+ Be sure to place your shopping cart in a return station when you're leaving.

THE GYM

A gym isn't a nightclub—hence the missing disco ball and lack of strobe lights. The gym is a place where health-minded people are striving to maintain or build upon their well-being, as well as enjoy a great workout and sense of accomplishment.

Here are a few tips to help you navigate the gym with ease and grace.

+ Leave your sunglasses in the car. You are at the gym, not walking the red carpet. So unless you are in the CIA or

witness protection program, save the shades for the
outdoors.

✦ Avoid using your cell phone. Not one person on the planet
  has ever gotten in shape by exercising their vocal chords.
  People don't want to hear about your tilted uterus or how
  your doctor, husband, or psychic is planning to fix it.

✦ The gym is not the spot for a coffee klatch. Keep moving
  after spin class and remember that the gym is a place to
  work out, not linger, and that most people are on a tight
  schedule.

✦ Your trainer is not your therapist. Trainers don't care about
  your best friend's bunion surgery, so let them do the job
  you are paying them to do.

✦ Refrain from giving unsolicited advice unless the gym's

general manager is paying your salary and insurance and contributing to your 401(k). If you suspect that someone is about to get hurt from using the equipment improperly, alert an employee of the gym, who can instruct the person on its proper use. A licensed trainer is the best solution for workout safety and positive results.

+ Keep grunts and loud moans to a minimum. You're working out, not birthing an eight-pound child.

+ Wait your turn: show other people respect while waiting around the cardio machines, locker room, water fountain, or the parking lot. Refrain from any outward signs of impatience—huffing, toe tapping, or furrowed brows. Remember, it's not only about how you look on the outside; your character, decorum, and kindness are what really make you shine.

+ Remember sweatiquette. Please, no sweat deposits! It's yours, so wipe it up and take it with you. Antiperspirant and deodorant keep sweat and stink at bay. So make them a staple of your workout.

+ If you pick something up, put it back! Ropes, balls, mats, and weights each belong in a special place. Leave things orderly for those who come after you.

+ Remember the three *S*'s: refrain from swearing, staring, or singing loudly to your amped-up iPod.

HOSPITAL VISITS

When going to visit a friend or family member in the hospital, call ahead to the nurses' station and ask for the food and flowers protocol, and find out if the patient has any allergies. Also ask about the nurses' favorite foods and bring something for them as well.

When you arrive at the hospital, make a pact with yourself to stay only ten to twenty minutes and an even shorter time if the patient has family visiting. Visitors from far away should get more visiting time.

At the elevator, press the call button with your elbow. Do the same once inside with the number panel. This will ensure that you aren't picking up any germs and bringing them into the room or home with you.

Make a brief stop at the nurses' station to drop off a small edible for them, ask if you can help them in any way, and also ask for any special instructions about visiting their patient.

The tips below will ensure a successful and uplifting visit to the hospital.

- Avoid wearing perfume or cologne. Strong perfumes often arrive before you do and linger long after you leave.
- Make sure that when you step off the elevator, you have a positive attitude and an arsenal of upbeat news to share. Walk in tall and cheerful, full of a willingness to listen. Don't overshare your latest kidney stone episode or your sister's elective cosmetic surgery, even if it is her fifth. This won't divert the patient, and the focus should stay on him or her.
- Take something that will please the patient and cheer the room, such as a favorite magazine, a potted plant with balloons attached, a book on audiotape, a picture drawn by a child in bold, bright colors with GET WELL splashed across the page, or a genuine "miss you" message.
- Don't plunk down on the bed as it will crowd the patient and could also interfere with any wires, tubes, etc., that the patient is hooked up to.
- If the patient has a roommate, be considerate by asking the roommate before turning on the TV, rearranging the seating, or opening hot, fragrant food. If you have a second, ask if the roommate needs anything—or would like privacy. If so, pull the curtain closed for them.
- Don't consume the patient's food—either what you brought or what the hospital delivers.
- If the doctors, nurses, or any other medical staff need to do anything, step out of the room to give the patient respect and privacy.

When leaving the hospital, make another brief stop at the nurses' station to thank them for all they do. Ask if they have any instructions for care of or visits to the patient once the patient is home. Sometimes patients need continued care once they leave the hospital, so it is important to have an accurate explanation of the necessary procedures from the medical professionals.

INTERNET CAFÉ AND WI-FI MANNERS

Café owners offer Wi-Fi to draw customers, but the Internet user has certain obligations when taking advantage of this.

+ Order something and also leave a tip since you are going to be using the café's real estate for a time.
+ Don't talk on the phone or text while ordering. Give the service staff 100 percent of your attention when placing your order. This way, you will more than likely receive exactly what you ordered and servers will not be left wondering if you are speaking to them or your cell phone buddy.
+ Don't snag a seat before you have placed an order. Show respect for the other people in line who are following protocol; order and pay first, and then choose a seat.
+ The condiment area is not a lounge, so don't hover there for ten minutes being a mixologist and making your coffee just right while other people are waiting and their coffee grows stale and cold. Also, clean up any spills and sugar packets and leave the area clean for the people who come after you.
+ Don't make your own breve or latte by ordering a shot of espresso and then adding the entire condiment containers of cream and milk.
+ If you are by yourself, do not choose the largest table in the cafe and spread yourself out. Leave the bigger tables for larger groups. Should only large tables be available, offer to share it with another Wi-Fi user.

- Be sure your laptop is charged before you arrive, since everyone will be vying for the outlet seats. If you have enough battery life for an hour or so, choose a seat without an outlet so someone else may use a seat with one.
- Keep your shoes on! If you prefer to work in your bare feet, then please work from home.
- For $1.95 you don't get unlimited Wi-Fi access and office space; buy something every couple of hours if you want to stay.
- Don't pester other customers with Wi-Fi questions; they are trying to work or relax and are not your on-site tech support.
- Never bring your own food. Wi-Fi is expensive for the establishment, so do your part and purchase something.
- Never leave your computer, phone, etc., and ask someone else to keep them on lockdown while you go to the restroom.

- Keep Internet stations open for Wi-Fi users. Read your magazines, books, and newspaper in non-Wi-Fi areas.
- Clean up your cups, papers, plates, and anything else you used.
- If you shift tables and chairs around, move them back to their original places when you are ready to pack it up. This shows consideration for the proprietor and also fellow customers.

MINGLE, MINGLE, MINGLE!

Do you feel awkward in social situations? Well, guess what? Over 90 percent of the clients I have worked with for the past twenty years have revealed they feel uncomfortable in social situations and at networking events, too. Let me show you how to navigate all things social, whether you are five or ninety-five, and improve your minglability.

- Go with the intention of making other people feel at ease. Since you now know that a large percent of the population is nervous and awkward in social situations, make it your job to help someone else feel more comfortable. It will take the pressure off how you are feeling about yourself.
- Remember people's names. When someone introduces himself, commit his name to memory and use it. In a social exchange, what sounds better? A simple "Nice to meet you" or "It is so nice to meet you, Tom"? Always use the person's name during the conversation. When we remember to say someone's name, it automatically puts them at ease. As simple as that, you are forming a new business relationship or personal friendship.
- Focus on building other people up. When someone tells you that they love the Bucs, the Yankees, or tiramisu, it's a perfect opportunity to engage, build rapport, and acknowledge the person speaking. It's a simple two-step process. Simply repeat what they told you, as in "So you

love the Yankees?" Then ask, "How long have you been a fan?" Just like that the other person feels heard, acknowledged, and important.

+ What do you talk about when you've already covered the traffic and the weather and there's a lull in the conversation? Bring up something topical that doesn't involve a scandal. I know, I know, it seems impossible to do, but you could talk about your last ski trip, a favorite restaurant, or the latest invention. Try to talk about positive things, such as children, pets, movies, music, books, sports, etc. Just remember it's a conversation, not an interrogation, so a nice balance should be kept between questions and answers from each person.

+ Avoid gossip of any sort. Don't do it yourself, and try to change the subject if someone else begins speaking negatively about another person. If people don't stop, explain how you don't have time to be critical of anyone else because you're too busy working on improving your own faults. Then move on to another subject.

MOVIE THEATERS

Cell phones are the number-one hecklers of our time. If you are at a movie theater, you know what to do—turn it off! Also, no text messaging—the light distracts people. And please don't take any screen shots: it isn't worth having security ask you to leave. If you have to text or you must make that phone call, take your anatomy outside the theater.

Following are a few more tips to take to the movies with you.

+ When entering a row of seats at the movie theater, face the people as you enter; your backside should be facing the screen. Remember to say "Excuse me" and "Thank you" while you locate your seat.

+ If a movie theater is sparsely filled, don't plunk down in front of someone. Choose a seat that isn't going to block anyone's view.

+ The movie doesn't need a narrator. All reviews, verbal anticipation of what will come next, or predictions about the end must be kept to yourself.

+ Try your best to sit once and remain seated. Get your food, drinks, and restroom stops taken care of before settling into your seat.

+ Bear in mind you have two hours, not two minutes, to consume your popcorn and other movie snacks. Try to pace yourself.

+ Children running up and down the aisles, crying, talking loudly, and announcing they have to go to the bathroom should not be part of the entertainment. When choosing to take little ones to the movies, be aware that others may have paid for a babysitter so they could enjoy a quite date night. If keeping your little angels quiet in the movie theater proves too daunting a task, then renting a movie to enjoy in the comfort of your home may be a better option until the kids are older and able to sit contentedly.

+ Coughing, hacking, sneezing, and wheezing are signs you should abstain from a trip to the movies. If you aren't well, do not expose others to germs or the sounds that sickness brings.

+ It's not 1956, and you're not at the drive-in theater, so no pawing, clawing, or tonsil hockey. The show is on the screen, not in your seat.

+ When the movie has ended and the credits are rolling, take a second to scan your immediate area for trash and dispose of it on the way out of the theater.

NEW NEIGHBORS

What do you do when someone new moves into your neighborhood? Well, once you see that moving truck pull away, wait a few days, then stop by for a brief and friendly visit. The goal is simple:

to extend a warm welcome by saying hello, exchanging information, and dropping off a welcome gift.

Many new-neighbor gift ideas are practical as well as welcoming. Here are just a few.

- A plate of warm cookies
- A plant
- An easy-to-prepare meal in a basket with gourmet red sauce and pasta, and a loaf of fresh Italian bread
- A menu organizer with all the area's best takeout menus. For an added touch, throw in a gift card to your favorite restaurant.
- Another helpful gift would be a new address book with all the area numbers that will be needed: dry cleaners, doctors, dentists, garbage pickup, electric company, babysitters, pet groomers, pet sitters, lawn services, pool cleaners, carpet cleaners, house cleaners, fitness center, deli, pharmacy, bakery, hairstylist.
- Stationery and a book of stamps
- Specialty teas and coffee
- Fresh fruit and vegetable basket
- If you really want to go out on a limb, a fun gift is a small birdfeeder and a package of birdseed. Now that's a gift that keeps on giving!

Never gossip about previous owners or other neighbors, and resist the urge to ask the new neighbors to cut the hedges or the grass, which might be in desperate need of attention. Trust that they will address the overgrowth once they are all settled in or that you can find a more appropriate time to bring it up later if they don't.

If you are the new neighbor and are the recipient of a new-neighbor welcome gift, be sure to send a thank-you note right away and invite those neighbors to your housewarming.

POOLSIDE

The pool is a wonderful place to have fun, exercise, or take shelter from the heat.

Below are a few tips to ensure a great day at the pool.

+ The number-one rule by the pool is safety. No glass, no running, and no oversunning.
+ Always bring sunscreen and apply it a minimum of three times per day—early morning, midday, and late afternoon.
+ Always be respectful of other people's peace. If you bring music (even if you bring your earbuds), don't jack that music to heaven. Keep it at a normal range.
+ If you get a cell phone call, please take it to a private part of the pool. No one wants to hear about your upcoming surgery while they are trying to relax.

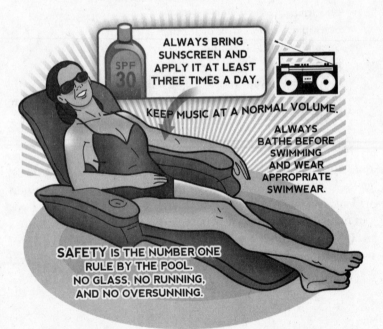

ALWAYS BRING SUNSCREEN AND APPLY IT AT LEAST THREE TIMES A DAY.

KEEP MUSIC AT A NORMAL VOLUME.

ALWAYS BATHE BEFORE SWIMMING AND WEAR APPROPRIATE SWIMWEAR.

SAFETY IS THE NUMBER ONE RULE BY THE POOL. NO GLASS, NO RUNNING, AND NO OVERSUNNING.

- Keep a close eye on your children. Don't become so relaxed that you let your guard down.
- Everyone has equal access to the pool. While swimming laps, doing water aerobics, or simply floating around, be mindful of other people.
- No one heads to the pool with the hopes of running into Sasquatch, so tame the savage body hair. With razors, Nair, laser hair removal, and electrolysis available today, it shouldn't take too long to groom yourself. This goes for men and women.
- No leering. Although being at the pool can be relaxing, it can also cause some people to feel self-conscious. It is one thing to admire beauty through your Ray-Bans, but no gawking or intense staring. Show some self-control.
- Bathe before swimming. Be sure to rinse off before jumping in to remove excess sunblock, lotions, oils, and sweat from sunbathing.
- Wear appropriate swimwear. Choose a suit that fits your body type. When you leave the pool and go through the common areas of a hotel, such as the lobby, you need to cover up. I am not saying you have to put on a burka over your bathing suit, but, please, be discreet.

SPAS

Spas are great places we visit to enjoy quiet time, tranquillity, and relaxation. Call to schedule services and ask for suggestions. When booking an appointment, let them know if you have a preference for a male or female massage therapist. If you are expecting Barbara and Bruno walks in to give you a massage, all pleasure and peace might be lost. If crowds make you nervous, book your appointments for during the week or off-peak hours. Make sure to let the staff know of any questions or concerns, so they will be able to book the perfect services and therapist for you.

Following are more tips to ensure a great day at the spa.

- Arrive twenty to thirty minutes early to relax, unwind, and double-check the starting times for your services. Do a walk-through or ask for a tour of where your appointments will be so you are familiar with where to go. Once you start your services and are all full of bliss, you don't want to get stressed-out looking for your next service location.
- Make sure you leave your cell phone in the car. You don't want to hear it ringing, and neither does anyone else. Remember, speak in hushed tones. Be quiet for your own relaxation and also for others'.
- Must you be in your birthday suit when you get a massage? It's your choice. If you want to wear undergarments, that's fine. It's a good idea to enjoy the sauna or the Jacuzzi prior to your services to help you relax. You can enjoy this in your bathing suit or without clothing in a single-sex spa room; either way, be discreet. Remember to take a fast, warm shower to rinse off chlorine and sweat before you head to your massage.
- Let your esthetician know about any skin sensitivities, medical conditions, or concerns that you might have. Share your preferences as to pressure, lighting, steams, pace, music, temperature, and products. Let the staff know how to make and keep you comfortable. At the end of the services, your therapist will say, "Take your time getting up." This lets you know that it's okay to rest for five minutes or so and enjoy the bliss. Just try not to take a full-blown nap!

The following things will make your day at the spa more enjoyable.

- Take a book and favorite magazines.
- Drink a lot of water after your service.
- Take water shoes for the shower.

- Eat a healthy meal and drink water two hours before services.
- Take breath mints—sometimes the therapist gets very close.
- Let your esthetician know if you are wearing contact lenses.
- Don't wear jewelry. It's a spa, not a cocktail party.
- Don't bring children or pets.
- Don't wear fragrance or perfume.
- Don't consume a heavy meal or drink alcohol before your services.
- Don't shave right before; leave at least two hours between shaving and a service.
- Don't talk about your angst and negative situations in your life; relax and think good thoughts.
- Tip 15 to 20 percent if the tip isn't already included.

TATTOO STUDIOS

You and your tattoo artist have the same goal: to create an amazing tattoo for you in the most painless way possible.

Once you have seen proof that the tattoo artist is licensed, look at their portfolio. If you want Tinker Bell on a tulip and all they do is skulls and crossbones, search for a different tattooist: they aren't the one for you.

Following are more tips to consider before getting a tattoo.

- Be aware that it takes time to draw and stencil a tattoo. If you don't have an appointment, be patient. The tattoo designer wants to give you ample time to create your artwork. If you aren't sure what type of tattoo you want, research a little more and come back another day. Don't make an impulsive choice since you'll have to live with it for a long time afterward.
- Some tattoo artists prefer not to be disturbed while working, so ask them their policy about conversation, and

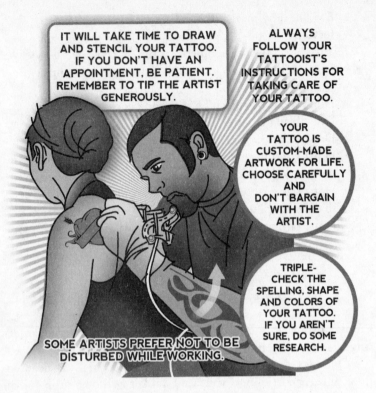

IT WILL TAKE TIME TO DRAW AND STENCIL YOUR TATTOO. IF YOU DON'T HAVE AN APPOINTMENT, BE PATIENT. REMEMBER TO TIP THE ARTIST GENEROUSLY.

ALWAYS FOLLOW YOUR TATTOOIST'S INSTRUCTIONS FOR TAKING CARE OF YOUR TATTOO.

YOUR TATTOO IS CUSTOM-MADE ARTWORK FOR LIFE. CHOOSE CAREFULLY AND DON'T BARGAIN WITH THE ARTIST.

TRIPLE-CHECK THE SPELLING, SHAPE AND COLORS OF YOUR TATTOO. IF YOU AREN'T SURE, DO SOME RESEARCH.

SOME ARTISTS PREFER NOT TO BE DISTURBED WHILE WORKING.

remember to shut off your cell phone before they start. You don't want to distract anyone poised over you with a needle. The studio isn't a place for children, so get a babysitter.

+ Once you've chosen your tattoo, no bargaining. You are not at a yard sale. They are giving you a custom-made artwork for life, so respect their pricing.

+ Triple-check the spelling, shape, and colors that you want on your tattoo.

+ Do you tip your tattoo artist? Absolutely. Twenty percent is standard.

+ Whatever you do, don't come in with a big ol' posse of people as your personal cheering section. Don't moan and scream and carry on as if you are birthing twins. It's a tattoo studio, not a maternity ward.

✦ Never, *ever* go into a tattoo studio if you've been drinking, or if you are stinking. You wouldn't want people to show up at your workplace in either condition.

✦ Be attentive to your tattooist's instructions for taking care of your tattoo. Proper care is needed to retain color, shape, health, and longevity of your tattoo. Keep the tattoo bandaged for the appropriate length of time, and keep it out of the sun, as the sun will discolor and fade it.

THE THEATER / PERFORMING ARTS CENTER

An evening at the theater can be a magical experience. The music, actors, musicians, and audience all come together for one goal—to have a memorable and spectacular evening. With so many people packed into one place, it's important to take common courtesy and respect along with your ticket when you go.

Following are some tips for visiting the theater.

✦ Have your tickets out and ready. Don't paw through your pocketbook or pockets to retrieve them. If you're with a large group of people, give them their own tickets for the doorman.

✦ Once you're inside, you may wonder, *Do I face the stage going into the row to my seat or do I face the people?* You always want to face the people, and as you pass them, look them in the eye and say hello, good evening, how are you, as well as pardon me and excuse me; do that all the way down until you find your seat.

✦ Being prompt at the theater means arriving fifteen to twenty minutes before the show is due to start. You want to have time to find your seat, read the program, and relax.

✦ Don't be a seat thief. I know you see those two seats down there twenty rows in front of you, and you're thinking nobody will ever know if you move down. But once you land in those seats, the people who had the flat tire are going to arrive and you'll have to do the hike of shame twenty rows back up; so sit in the seat you've bought.

✦ Be respectful and don't talk, whisper, sing, or hum during the performance. You can be sure you aren't what the other guests came to hear and see.

✦ Don't use your atomizer before going to the theater. People didn't come to the theater for aromatherapy, or an allergic reaction. Many people are allergic to fragrances, so make sure scent isn't a part of your outfit when you depart for the theater.

✦ Remember the three C's: no cameras (or video), no cell phones, and no candy (or gum). If you forgot to get rid of that sweet treat before the show, just put it in a piece of tissue in your purse or pocket.

✦ Applaud. Performers appreciate when patrons applaud enthusiastically, shout "Bravo," and give standing ovations. It is appropriate to applaud after a well-performed song or dance, after each scene or act, and at curtain call.

✦ At the end of the show when all the actors come out, the protocol for the curtain call is to clap and show them your appreciation. I know your bunions are barking and your Spanx are pinching, but stay and show those actors the love. They need to see your pride and not your backside.

THEME PARKS

Vacation theme parks are a highlight of summer. Here are a few dos and don'ts to help you navigate, enjoy, and make the most of your day at an amusement park.

✦ Map out your day of adventure the night before, so you can plan for the attractions that most interest all members of your party.

✦ Try your best to arrive at the theme park right when it

opens. Get there early so you can enjoy the rides, the shows, and the food before the masses breeze in.

+ Jot down the location of your vehicle (the section, row, and lane that you parked in) so you don't roam around at the end of the day like a gladiator in search of your chariot.

+ Theme parks are the least crowded in the early morning and the late afternoon, so plan your day accordingly. Mealtimes—noon and five P.M.—are most crowded in restaurants. You will experience less waiting if you take your meals before or after these high-traffic times.

+ Don't forget sunscreen, and apply at least three times a day—early morning, lunchtime, and late afternoon, and more frequently if you use a sunscreen with a low SPF.

+ Do take your photos in designated picture-taking locations, not in the middle of busy walkways or in the stream of the crowds headed to the biggest theme-park attractions.

+ Respect the ride attendants! Know the number of guests in your party and tell the staff promptly so they can get you on and off the rides quickly. Remember to make eye contact while thanking them when you get on and off the ride.

+ Remember that personal space is important. Always keep a distance of three feet—approximately the length of a yardstick—from other people when possible. The three-foot rule doesn't apply to lines, but do your best to keep a comfortable distance from other people while waiting to board rides.

+ Bathing suits are for the beach, pools, and the Miss America pageant. If you aren't a contestant, please leave your bathing suit at home.

+ Keep it clean! Treat the amusement park the way you would your own property. Make it nice for the folks who arrive after you. If you must smoke, do so in the designated areas and dispose of your cigarette butts properly.

TIPS ON TIPPING

The holidays are a wonderful time to show appreciation to the people who grace our lives with their talents. Give special gifts to these people between November 25 and December 25; the earlier the better!

By giving a monetary or material gift (or both) to the people who have made our lives easier throughout the year, we let them know how much we appreciate what they have done for us.

If possible, give the gift in person. If you are giving money, never give it raw and in the open as if you were greasing the palm of a Mafia don. Enclose it in a card with a handwritten note of appreciation.

Here are some guidelines to help navigate the confusing world of tipping, gift giving, and showing gratitude throughout the holiday season.

+ Letter carrier/package courier: $20 gift card
+ Hairdresser: double tip or full cost of session
+ Manicurist: $15 to $20 (or $25 if they work on your scary toes)
+ Housekeeper: full dollar amount of one cleaning
+ Lawn service/gardener: $20
+ Pool cleaner: full dollar amount of one cleaning
+ Nanny: one week's pay and a small gift from child
+ Teenage babysitter: small gift from child or $15 iTunes gift card
+ Newspaper delivery person: $10 to $15
+ Trainer, massage therapist, or yoga instructor: amount of one full session
+ Trash collector: $10 to $15 per person
+ Pet groomer: ranges from double tip to amount of full session
+ Dog walker/pet sitter: full amount of one or two sessions
+ Teachers: one of your *kidneys*! Even if you already gave one to your hairdresser!

Happy holidays!

TOBACCONIST TIPS FOR THE CIGAR ENTHUSIAST

When smoking and enjoying a cigar, remember to always be considerate of other people. Be conscious of how the cigar smoke might affect the people around you. That goes for cigarette smoking as well. Even people who don't routinely smoke cigars may celebrate an engagement or the birth of a child with one.

Following are a few tips to help navigate the world of cigars.

- Not sure which cigar to choose? Ask the tobacconist for suggestions and favorites.
- To prepare a cigar for smoking, cut it just above the cap line using a double-edge guillotine.
- When lighting your cigar, first warm the tobacco at the foot (or the end you don't put in your mouth) by rotating or twirling it between two fingers for about a minute.
- Use a butane lighter or wooden matches. Paper matches can leave a chemical taste.
- Place the cigar in your mouth. Strike a match and hold the flame beneath the foot of the cigar and slightly puff. Enjoy the taste and aroma, remembering to never inhale.
- Hold the cigar between your thumb and index finger or index and middle fingers. Both ways are acceptable.
- Once the cigar has been lit for a few minutes, you can remove the band. The heat will loosen the glue on the band, allowing it to be easily removed.
- Relax and enjoy your cigar. It should take about sixty minutes to finish. Taking one puff a minute will help keep it lit.
- Pair a full-bodied cigar with a full-bodied drink such as cognac or scotch. A lighter cigar is often nice with champagne or a nonalcoholic drink. Coffee and espresso are excellent choices to team up with cigars as well.
- Retire your cigar after smoking about two-thirds of it.
- Be sure not to fondle and smell multiple cigars. If you do need to smell one, simply take in the aroma from the foot of the cigar.
- When cutting your cigar, don't use your teeth. If you don't have a cigar-cutter, use a Swiss Army knife.
- Be certain not to slobber on, chew, or bite your cigar. If the tip of the cigar gets soggy, the taste and aroma will soon become stale.
- Do not gesture or point with your cigar.
- Don't let the flame ever touch the wrapper, which is the

outermost leaf layer of the cigar. Rotate the cigar's foot closely above the flame, but never let them touch.

+ Don't dip your cigar in cognac or any other beverage, as it will compromise the taste and aroma.
+ Don't crush your cigar as if it were a cigarette when you are finished; it will leave a foul odor. Just let it rest in an ashtray for two minutes and it will automatically go out.
+ Don't chain-smoke cigars. Wait at least fifteen to twenty minutes between cigars.

THE ZOO

Whether at the zoo or on the Serengeti Plain, rules are there for your protection and also for the protection of the animals. The first thing we usually want to do when we see an animal is feed it. People food and any other small little treat can cause stomach problems for the animals. So unless you're in a designated feeding area and dispensing official food, please do not feed the animals.

Here are a few more zoo policies you will want to follow.

+ Refrain from throwing anything into the animals' habitats; even the tiniest of objects can be hazardous.
+ Stay on designated walkways. Remember, the fences are there for your safety.
+ This may be hard to believe, but some people are cruel to animals without even knowing it. For instance, when visiting snake enclosures, people sometimes tap on the glass. Since snakes can't hear, they respond to the movement by striking the glass and hurting their mouths; so no glass tapping!
+ Keep fingers, toes, arms, and other body parts away from fence openings. Keep children three feet back from the glass and barriers.
+ Loud and unruly behavior stresses the animals, so keep your voice low and sudden movements to a minimum.

- When taking photos, make sure you aren't leaning into the animal enclosures or blocking anyone's view.
- Help children be respectful of the landscape by keeping them from picking flowers, climbing trees, and running on sectioned-off grass.
- Keep a watchful eye on your kids and have an emergency plan if they end up out of your sight. Here is the quick three-step emergency plan: (1) Don't wander away from a place once you are lost. Alert a female uniformed employee and tell her you are lost. Tell your child this once inside the park; if they should get lost, point to whom they would ask for help. (2) Wear bold colors—bright orange or bold pink. Dress alike in these bright colors. (3) Make sure your child has memorized both parents' cell phone numbers, and also write them in the tongue of their shoes and tags of their shirt.
- Make sure all trash is placed in trash cans or recycling bins. Help keep the zoo beautiful and clean for the people who visit after you.

Twelve

SPORTS

Professional Baseball Blunders

One of the best things about being an etiquette coach is that it takes me to all kinds of fascinating and wonderful places. Last year I found myself sitting in the offices of a professional baseball team. I was helping them with some social media and business etiquette branding, and the manager asked me what was the best way to get the players not to text during team meetings and practices. The team wasn't playing well and was making lots of mental errors on the field. The manager knew the players had talent and physical ability, but they just weren't putting it together.

Several times during my visit with the manager, I noticed that the team's pitching coach was looking down at texts or sending e-mails. I suspected that this was where the problem might have been coming from, so I asked to sit in for fifteen minutes at the next team meeting.

A week later I observed a team meeting, and before long I saw that I'd been correct: the pitching coach was texting while the manager was speaking. No matter where you are or what you do, people are watching. They will notice your inattention, even if you're just glancing down and checking a text.

My advice was that the other coach shouldn't glance down at his phone, not even once during the meetings. The team's texting problems soon went away, and the coach banned phones from player meetings and the dugout.

With that same team, I also attended a private coaches' meeting to try to decide which of two players to bring up from the minor leagues. The players were both vastly talented, smart, and offered tremendous promise to the organization. When the scouts mentioned that one of the players was on his phone constantly and texting excessively during the day, it sent a red flag to management.

The team eventually went with the player who was more alert and respectful during one-on-one face time.

It may not be the big things but the little things that people remember.

CHAMPIONSHIP GAME PARTIES: SUPER BOWL / WORLD SERIES / ETC.

No matter what sport you enjoy watching, the most exciting games of the season are the championship games. Many people like to host parties for these events, such as the Super Bowl, World Series, Stanley Cup, NBA Finals, World Cup, etc.

Here are a few tips whether you enjoy one or all sports.

+ Ask the host what you can bring. If they say nothing, bring a party food anyway for all to enjoy. Make sure it is something you can just pick up and eat without needing utensils, such as wings, bean dip with chips, cupcakes, etc. Everyone will want to have plenty to munch on while cheering on their favorite team.

+ These are some of the year's biggest events, coupled with the year's biggest buffets, so no fat-free foods or talk of dieting.

+ No double-dipping the chips. Do not be found hovering over the buffet as if someone is about to snatch it away. Pace yourself, since you'll be watching the game for a couple hours or more.

+ When choosing where to sit for the game, wait to see where the hosts sit, then take a seat. They worked hard to put the party together for everyone, so make sure they get good seats for the game.

+ If you want to get invited to the next championship game, be a great guest. At the end of each quarter, inning, or half, walk around and pick up orphaned cups, plates, and napkins. Help with keeping things neat and clean throughout the evening. Ask the hosts if there is anything they would like you to do or not do.

+ It's great to be excited at the game and show lots of team spirit, but watch your conduct. If your team is trailing, don't act all crazy. Chances are the players are not a part of your family and the team is not contributing to your 401(k), so keep your disappointment to yourself and try to be philosophical.

+ When the game is over, help with the cleanup and then go home. It's not New Year's Eve, so no need to stay until the next day.

+ Don't forget to thank the hosts for inviting you; let them know what a great time you had, even if your team came in second.

GOLF

Golf etiquette is an essential part of the game. Some policies are in place for the safety of the golfers, others to keep the game enjoyable for all players, and a few for maintaining the quality of the course.

If you are a newcomer to the game or just need a quick brushup on your golfing manners, below are some basic guidelines that will help keep the game pleasurable for you and those around you.

+ Be respectful of other golfers' schedules by showing up on time or even a little early for your tee time or lesson with the golf pro.

+ Be sure to leave your cell phone in the car, but if you must

have it with you, put it on vibrate. You don't want it to go off when someone is in the middle of their backswing. If you absolutely have to accept or make a call, be considerate and move away from the other players and keep the conversation short.

✦ Be prepared to play when it is your turn. You don't want to take your turn slowly and hold up all the other golfers. If you lose your ball, never spend more than five minutes looking for it.

✦ Do not allow your golf cart to leave a trail of carnage. Avoid wet areas where the cart will damage the turf, and don't feel as though you must play follow the leader if the path in front of you is torn up. You will make matters worse.

- Repair the ground after your shot by fixing ball marks and divots, and rake the sand in the bunker smooth. It's hard enough to get out of a sand trap; you certainly don't want someone else's ball to land in your footprint because you forgot to rake.
- If you have a temper, keep it under control on the course. Never let your club go flying over the green because you are unhappy with your last shot, and no sulking or foul language. Frustrating moments are a given in golf—so find a way to vent in a nonoffensive way.
- When other players are getting ready to take a shot, remain quiet and still so as not to distract them. Talking, taking practice swings, or walking around in their line of vision can really break their concentration.
- Help your fellow players by looking for lost balls, picking up clubs they have left on the fringe, or gathering up head covers stranded near the tee.
- Encourage each other by saying, "Nice shot," whenever warranted.
- Be observant on the course and pick up other etiquette tips. The more you practice good golf manners, the more you will be treated with the same level of respect.

NASCAR

NASCAR stands for National Association for Stock Car Auto Racing. Forty-two or more different teams and drivers are in NASCAR. Whether you're sitting in the grandstands or camping out in the infield, help assure that a good time will be had by all.

To get the best seats, call as soon as tickets go on sale. Consider a season-purchase a year in advance. Other options include buying tickets from the track Web sites, or searching your local newspaper. Good-choice Web sites include hub.com, Craigslist, and eBay.

NASCAR is best enjoyed from the grandstands, and not the front row. The best seats are the highest seats, which isn't usually the case in other major sporting events. Sitting up in the higher seats gives a full view of the track, while sitting in the lower seats gives you a view of cars zooming by in a blur.

Below are more tips to get the most out of your day at the track.

+ Keep in mind that grandstand tickets usually sell out first.
+ The infield (inside track) is like a major tailgate party at a college football game. Fans arrive in their motor homes, cars, and campers and even bring tents to pitch.
+ To cheer for your favorite driver, know their car number. Well-seasoned, die-hard NASCAR fans refer to the team or driver by number.
+ Necessities for a great day at the races are sunscreen, a pocket raincoat (in case of a rain delay), sunglasses, wet wipes, Chap Stick, cushions (sporting your driver's car number and logo, of course), and a camera. Also, don't forget cash to avoid potentially long ATM lines. For safety reasons, glass or mammoth coolers are not permitted. It is a good idea to call ahead to ask about the standard cooler size and other track policies.
+ "Think green" for a clean track. Use trash cans instead of throwing any items toward or on the track.
+ Visit the concession stands before the race starts and during caution times.
+ Be respectful of a driver who is involved in an accident; no clapping or cheering.
+ If you find yourself sitting next to a novice race fan, give them a hand up. Whether you're five or ninety-five, it is never too late to learn about NASCAR.
+ Monitor your alcohol intake so you don't do crazy things that may get you a free escort out of the racetrack.
+ Keep your verbiage clean and appropriate. Children may be in the stands within earshot of your adult language.
+ When the race begins, the first or front car isn't a part of

the race, it's the pace car. This vehicle sports advertising for the track and is usually the innovative car of the year. It leads the pack of racers to a clean start.

+ Garage passes/credentials for the races are like backstage passes for a concert. These get you a behind-the-scenes peek at the garage area and a look at what's going on in the pits before the race starts. Garage passes are usually for family, friends, and members of race teams or people who are affiliated with NASCAR.

+ The garage pass gives a close-up view of the crews getting ready for the big race; you can also get a glimpse of the drivers as they're going to their cars. The crews are busy making sure that all is well with the car, team, pit crew, and driver. Don't touch things, and be careful not to get in the way. Long pants, closed-toe shoes, and a shirt that covers your shoulders are mandatory.

+ If you want an autograph from a driver, bring your own black Sharpie and have your program open or your item ready to hand to the driver. Also, if you walk with drivers, don't try to get them to stop. It's much easier to get an autograph while they are moving; they may not want to stop for fear of being mobbed. Always use the magic words *please* and *thank you* when asking for an autograph. Don't expect to have a full-blown dialogue with the driver, as he has his mind on racing.

+ The flags. The green flag is waved to start the race. A red flag means all cars must stop. Yellow means caution: all drivers must slow down. The white flag indicates the last lap of the race. The driver who gets a black flag must get off the track immediately. Finally, when the black-and-white checkered flag is waved, the winning car has crossed over the finish line.

+ Focus on cheers and not jeers for a race well done.

POKER

Whether playing at home or in a casino, online or live, some basic rules of behavior should be followed by all players.

- Be polite to the dealer. They are not psychics, so be respectful regarding the cards dealt, whether good or bad. Show respect toward your fellow players: no outbursts, verbal sparring, or profanity.
- Play at a reasonable speed. You may have to take a little extra time now and then, but don't deliberate over every move; it slows the pace and momentum.
- Play in turn. Never leave your seat or fold your hand unless it's your turn to bet, as you could be giving away valuable information to another player. When you do decide to fold, make sure the cards are facedown when you give them to the dealer, handle them gently, and never throw them or slap them down on the table.
- Don't splash the pot by throwing in your chips as if you're playing horseshoes. Stack them neatly so the dealer can reach and count them. If you sling them into the middle, it's difficult to determine if enough chips have been pushed in. If you are on a winning streak and want to pocket a few chips to ensure you walk away with something, think twice. All chips must stay on the table until the end.
- Don't coach other players or morph into sportscaster Jim Nantz and comment; others are concentrating. This rule applies to cell phone use and texting as well. Keep all distractions to a minimum. Even body language can distract or reveal things you don't want your opponent to know.

SKYBOXES

Part of the fun and excitement of going to a sporting event is to hear the cheers of the crowd and be in the middle of the action.

Being invited to sit in an elevated skybox at the stadium allows for this same enjoyment, while also providing luxury, privacy, space to move around, and no obstructions.

Other names for the skybox are luxury, private, corporate, and executive box. Skyboxes are generally paid for by a corporation and are sometimes used for corporate events. These are usually by invitation only, to bring together clients or to reward employees who perform well. Skyboxes can also be leased for private parties.

Most skyboxes have comfortable seats, a small kitchen, and a bar. Others can be even more elaborate, with comfortable couches, a big-screen TV, climate control, windows that open to the stadium, a private bathroom, and other amenities. The more bells and whistles, the more expensive it is to lease or buy.

Additional perks of being invited to a skybox may include reserved parking and a special entrance and exit away from the crowds. Also, food is catered. Instead of a hot dog and beer, the fare is more sophisticated and may be paired with champagne or fine wine. A bartender or server will likely be on call to meet the needs of the guests.

Below are some guidelines so you get the maximum pleasure from your skybox experience.

+ Skybox seating is in close quarters, so forgo the additional spritzing. Some people may be allergic to perfumes, and you don't want to spoil the event for anyone.
+ Greet your host upon arrival and thank them when leaving.
+ Make sure you get there on time, then ask the host if they need any help.
+ Never plunk yourself down in any ol' seat. Wait for the host to tell you where to sit, or let the host and their family sit first, as well as higher-ranking people if it is an office gathering. They should be allowed the best seats.
+ Don't talk too much or too loudly and never use profanity.
+ If the skybox has a bathroom, use it for quick visits only. Should you need the bathroom longer than a minute or

two, venture out into the arena and utilize the public
restrooms, as you want to show respect for the other
skybox patrons and your host. You wouldn't want to do
anything to offend them or embarrass yourself.

+ Don't be a skybox jack-in-the-box. Refrain from passing
in front of others too much and possibly hindering their
view. You don't want anyone to miss a good play.

+ Don't overindulge in food or alcohol. The food may be
complimentary for you, but it's not a free-for-all.

+ Never invite your friends in regular stadium seating into
another person's skybox. One more person does matter, as
the host is charged per head for food and drinks.

+ If you do have a coveted front seat in a skybox, after an
hour or so you can offer the seat to someone else.

- If you notice that only one item of any kind remains (whether food, beverage, or dessert), don't grab it. First ask if anyone else would like it; if not, then you may enjoy.
- Always tip the suite attendant. This honors your host, the servers, and the stadium. If you are uncertain of the amount, ask someone on the service staff.
- After you have enjoyed the sporting event, taken pleasure in the catered food and drinks, and even benefited from having your parking paid for, send the hosts a thank-you note. Let them know how much you appreciated being invited to the game and what a great time you had.

Skyboxes may not be for everyone; everyday sports fans might prefer stadium seating so they can be within shouting distance of their favorite team, rough it up with other fans, and enjoy hot dogs, beer, and chips. If you've never have the opportunity to enjoy an event from a skybox, keep in mind that most stadiums give free tours so you can glimpse how sports fans from the elite watch games.

STADIUMS

Attending sporting events can be loads of fun and exciting for the sports enthusiast. When visiting a stadium, remember the following rules to ensure a good time is had by all.

- Always have your tickets out and ready to give to the ticket taker. No holding up the line while excavating those tickets from the bottom of your backpack or pocketbook.
- When you're walking to your seat, be patient. Don't barge and zigzag your way through the crowd; walk with the multitude.
- During the national anthem, place your hand over your heart and take your hat off. It is truly the time to be 100 percent respectful.
- When you want to get a stadium vendor's attention, no yelling, "Yo, dawg, over here!" Simply raise your arm and

the vendor will come to you. If you're in the middle of a row and have to ask people to pass your food and money, be sure to thank them.

+ Inside the stadium is a "no-heckle zone." Remember to stand only for exciting moments and plays, and that goes for cheering, too. If you feel the urge to stand or cheer through an entire game, move to an area where people aren't sitting behind you.

+ Every town has a Cooter Brown. That's the person who drinks too much and always ends up acting crazy. Don't get "Cootered" at the game.

+ No cursing. Keep what you say intelligent and kind. Besides, children or clergymen may be sitting behind you.

+ Leave cell phones in the car to keep you from morphing into Bob Costas (the American sportscaster) and giving your cousin in Iowa a play-by-play.

+ When you see celebrities or family members of a player, no stalking them. Don't even eyeball them. Leave them be. But if you just can't help it and have to say hello, be brief while remembering the three-foot rule—stand at least three feet away from whomever you are speaking with.

TAILGATING

When you think about tailgating, the first thing that comes to mind is food, drinks, and laughing with old and new friends while you await the big game. Football has rules so that the game can be played with (you hope) a winning outcome. The same thing applies to tailgating.

Enjoy the people, the music, the game, and all the fun that comes with them. But the best thing about tailgating is sampling and sharing all the food and drinks. Be sure you pack enough to dole out and share.

Below are a few tips to make your tailgating all the fun it's intended to be.

+ Make a list and check it twice. Prepare the day before.
+ Arrive three to four hours before the event, scout out your spot, and set up camp.
+ Tailgating is one big potluck festival, so make enough for others.
+ Use resealable storage bags for your meat. The bags keep meat airtight and are easy to dispose of after the event.
+ Don't be a moocher. You don't want to show up with just a smile. Offer to bring something and bring plenty.

- Don't jack up your music to the high heavens. Noise can pollute, too.
- Set up with like-minded tailgaters, people who share your interests.
- Pack emergency items such as a flashlight, first-aid kit, rain gear, can opener, and toilet paper.
- If you fly an American flag, show respect. If you opt to fly other flags, always remember that the American flag sits highest, and don't fly it after dark.
- When you're ready to break down your camp, make sure to be a safe grill master by being triple sure your coals are cool before you dispose of them; to cool quicker, poor water over the coals.
- Bring trash bags and clean up your gathering area. Try to leave it better than you found it.

TENNIS

The basic goal of tennis is to hit the little, optic-yellow ball diagonally across the net so well that your opponent doesn't have a prayer of hitting it back. If you're courtside and a match is going on, talk quietly so as not to distract the players. Also, if a point is in play, don't cross behind the court. Wait for the point to finish, then cross quickly before play resumes.

Here are a few tips when playing tennis.

- Court time for singles is about an hour; doubles is about an hour and a half. If you get to your reserved court and people are finishing up a game, no pacing or grunting, just be respectful and give them time to finish.
- When you're ready to play, place your racquet cover, can of balls, and jacket off to one side.
- Warm-up is important for you and your opponent to help prevent injuries. Keep in mind, it's not practice, so hit the ball to your opponent at a reasonable pace.
- To determine who is going to serve, you can do a racquet

spin or a coin toss. The winner decides if they're going to receive or serve.

- ✦ The server should call the score before each serve. This will ensure that you and your opponent are on the same wavelength and avoid disputes.
- ✦ Do not return serves that are obviously long or wide. This is considered rude. Just hit the ball into the net in front of you or let it lie near the fence behind you.
- ✦ If the receiver is not ready, they should not make any attempt at the ball but simply say, "I wasn't ready." If you go after the ball and then state you were not ready, you're out of luck.
- ✦ Always respect your opponent's line calls. If you're wondering whether your opponent's shot is out or in, it's in!
- ✦ Spectators should not applaud missed shots or double faults, and you should not heckle the opposing player.
- ✦ If your opponent wins, be sure to congratulate him. If he loses, be sure to thank him for an amazing game. No matter what kind of game you're having, never be crotchety. Always be positive; no one wants to play with a disgruntled player. I tell my little boys, "Your body does what your mouth says," so be positive and cordial, and fun will surely follow.

TRIATHLONS

The best thing a triathlete can do for fellow participants is set a good example: your actions speak volumes.

Here are several tips to follow to ensure the best results for everyone.

WHILE TRAINING
- ✦ Make sure you show up on time for all scheduled group swims, rides, and runs; it's not polite to keep others waiting.

- Ask your workout partners to choose the route and be careful not to push yourself or anyone else too hard.
- Don't turn your workouts into races unless you and your training partners have agreed upon this. Why train with someone if you are continually pulling ahead of them and ending up alone anyway?
- Don't whine or complain. This will only bring others down and make them wish they hadn't joined you for a workout. Keep conversations positive and fun.

SWIM

- If a swimmer is in a lane, always ask permission to share before getting into the pool. If you are unable to ask face-to-face because the swimmer is already doing laps, then sit with your legs in the water or stand in the left corner of the lane until the swimmer is aware that you are entering their lane.
- If two swimmers are sharing a lane, there is no need to circle swim. If there are more than two swimmers, circle swim counterclockwise.
- Don't use hand paddles when sharing a lane with other swimmers unless everyone in the lane is using them.
- When you want to get ahead of another swimmer in your lane, gently tap their toes, then swiftly pass in front of them. Don't attempt to pass unless you are sure you can comfortably overtake the other swimmer and maintain your speed.

BIKE

- Ride single file if possible for the safety of all the cyclists.
- Never use an iPod when riding unless you are on a stationary bike.
- If you are slowing down for any reason, be sure to yell out, "Braking," to warn other cyclists, and use signals to point out hazards, such as oncoming cars and traffic lights.

✦ Do not spit when riding with a group. If you absolutely must, pull away from the pack.

RUN

✦ On a trail, all slower runners and walkers should stay to the right. If you are going to pass someone, do so on their left and warn them, saying, "I'm approaching your left" or "I'm passing on the left."

✦ Running with your dog can be fun, but be sure to keep him on a short leash so he doesn't get tangled up with other people working out or walking their pets.

✦ If you are running or walking on a track and are slower than the other runners, be sure to stay in the outside lane, leaving the inside lanes for faster runners.

✦ Be responsible for your own water and gel packs. Don't ask your training partner to carry things for you just because they have pockets and you don't.

RACE DAY

✦ Read the race rules in advance of the race and be sure to observe them on race day. Know the route for each leg of the race to prevent confusion and possible injuries from trying to backtrack.

✦ Do not use an iPod during the race; it is hazardous to you and the other athletes.

✦ Do not place your bike or any other equipment on top of or too close to another participant's gear in the transition area. Be respectful of the other athletes and their equipment.

✦ Everyone trained hard for this event, so don't distract others with idle chatter. Respect that many will want to stay focused.

✦ Although your pets may be used to hanging out with you, they should stay home on race day. You do not need the distraction and neither do the other athletes.

+ Keep the course neat and clean by not littering. Throw your used gel packs, water bottles, etc., in the trash cans provided.

SWIM

+ If you know you are a slower swimmer, stay toward the back or outside of the crowd at the starting line so the faster swimmers don't end up swimming on top of you.
+ Don't slap, push, pull, or crowd other swimmers during the swim.

BIKE

+ When cycling, always stay to the right side of the course unless you are passing another rider, and keep as straight a line as possible.
+ If you are about to pass someone, yell, "Passing on your left," to alert the rider ahead of you. Once you pass and are far enough ahead of the rider behind you, get back to the right and in a straight line.
+ If your bike should break down in any way, be sure to get off the race course to the right.
+ Dispose of any trash and empty water bottles at the aid stations.

RUN

+ Keep to the right during the run unless you are going to pass someone.
+ As you pass other runners, be sure to say something encouraging to them.
+ When approaching the aid stations, be careful: watch out for water cups, gel packs, and bottles dropped on the ground.
+ Make room for everyone at the aid station to get a drink, then quickly get back on the course.

EVERYDAY ETIQUETTE

POST-RACE

- ✦ Crossing the finish line can be incredibly emotional, but don't be too dramatic. Some may view this as unsportsmanlike behavior.
- ✦ Immediately go to a volunteer for removal of your race chip.
- ✦ Move away from the finish line to make room for the other finishers and get yourself a bottle of water.
- ✦ Treat the event coordinators and volunteers with respect. You may have finished the race, but they still have a lot of work to do.
- ✦ Once you have somewhat recovered, go and cheer on the other competitors, and socialize with the other athletes.
- ✦ No matter what your results, be a good sport. Smile at others, hold your head high, and be proud of your accomplishments.
- ✦ Before leaving, try to find the race directors and thank them for the hard work they put into organizing the event.

Thirteen

ENCOURAGEMENT IN TOUGH TIMES

Small and Subtle Acts

Many people do not know what to do, what to say, or how to act to give encouragement in tough times. We (myself included) sometimes overthink what to do and say. We need to let brevity be our guide. For example, at a funeral we can say one comforting sentence to the grieving person and save the other things for a nice letter sent a few weeks later. During one of the most hurtful times of my life, a small, silent act of kindness was the perfect thing.

I was ten years old when my mother passed away. The rain trickled down as my mother's friends, coworkers, and people from church stopped by our house to pay their respects. They all looked at me as if they were more confused and dazed than I was. I know that each person who stopped by the house that rainy morning wanted to comfort me and my siblings. But what I most remember is being confused by their confusion.

My uncle came into the den, walked right up to me, picked me up, and just held me for the longest time. He didn't say a thing. That was the most perfect slice of kindness I could ever have been given.

So many of us worry about what we're going to say or what we're going to do when people pass away, lose a job, divorce, or have to send their teenage or adult child to rehab. Simple, small acts of kindness are always the best bet: an "I'm thinking of you," a squeeze of the hand, or a comforting hug. I'm well aware that you can't hoist up your grieving boss the way my uncle held me, but if we are prepared when hardships hit, we won't be as awkward in our efforts to comfort and give help.

BAD NEWS AND HOW TO HANDLE IT

At times, a friend, coworker, or relative of yours will have to deal with a difficult situation. Offer your encouragement and help the person weather the storm of emotions. Following are some tips to help you know what to say and do in delicate situations.

DIVORCE / BREAKUP

+ Nod and listen when being told about the split. Tell the person you will be there for them as they go through this.
+ Never talk negatively about the other person; it's tantamount to saying your friend lacks sound judgment.
+ Don't ask questions about future living arrangements or who gets the house.
+ Let them know you are ready to listen anytime, day or night.
+ Think about them on holidays and make sure they have a place to go. Comfort them if their children will be with the spouse.
+ Send notes of encouragement and offer to meet them for coffee, a movie, or a sporting event.
+ Don't ask questions that may seem too sensitive or offensive, such as "Was he/she having an affair?"
+ Be sure not to make any unfavorable comments about your friend's appearance—for instance, that they are looking tired, stressed, or "not themselves."
+ Refrain from sharing any negative divorce news—for instance, that your sister is losing everything but her clothes, or that your brother is having to ride a skateboard to work because his ex got the car.

DRUG REHABILITATION OF A CLOSE FRIEND OR RELATIVE

+ Remark on their bravery for taking a bold step to face the truth and get better.
+ Use encouraging words about the future being better,

more successful, and that you will be thinking of them. Share that you are optimistic about a quick and successful recovery.

+ Never make a diagnosis, share autobiographical stories, or offer remedies. Rehabilitation should be left in the hands of trained professionals.
+ Don't walk on eggshells around the person. Keep it light, be supportive, and now and then a little humor is appreciated.
+ Never underestimate the power of just closely listening, offering a kind word and a heartfelt hug.

JOB LOSS OR BANKRUPTCY

At some time in all of our lives, we will be fired, laid off, or simply have to quit a job. You can thrive and survive the emotional transition from working to being out of work. Start by giving yourself twenty-one to thirty days to absorb the shock. Gather your emotions and regain your footing so you can make a strong game plan for landing back in the job market. Whether the job loss was deserved or unwarranted, it is a blow to your emotions. Refocus by eating well, working out, journaling, and building a foundation for your business plan to return to work. Your goal is to be emotionally stable, well rested, and physically ready.

Following are some steps to get yourself ready to jump back into the job market.

+ Journaling for twenty minutes a day or more about disillusionment, anger, unfairness, shock, etc., is a good way to let emotions out and helps with moving forward. Also, list what you're grateful for. First thing in the morning, get that journal out and have your way with it.
+ Make sure to work out. When we are healthy, we feel better and look better. Working out causes positive changes and can transform some of the negative thoughts and emotions that come with a job loss. Even walking thirty to

forty-five minutes a day produces amazing physical and mental results.

+ Make and keep a tight schedule every day. Get up at the same time and follow through with your goals of eating well, journaling, and working out, then block off three to four hours to start job searching. Keep that schedule five days a week and don't deviate. Doing this will help to alleviate fear and anxiety. Keeping a business schedule lets your mind and body know you are on track. Falling prey to nonproductive activities, such as watching TV, ranting, sleeping late, wasting too much time on social media, and so forth, makes you feel worse.

+ Get all your contacts in order and go through your business cards. Also, get your résumé updated for distribution. The résumé is still an important tool in the job market, but not as important as your online brand or persona. So google yourself and see what surfaces. Make sure you have up-to-date profiles on LinkedIn, Facebook, and Twitter, as this is where potential employers are going to really find out about you. Your picture should be the same on every social networking site for consistency. Make sure your contact information and phone numbers are easy to find and current; be certain your cell phone message is professional and without any techno-funk beat. Get a new business card with your current information.

+ You can improve your Google ranking by blogging about your expertise in your field—making sure to put in key words that are used in your field. Also search on Google for some tips on how to improve your presence in Google results.

+ Contacting headhunters, employment agencies, and friends will also be valuable in your job search. Be sure to ask people who were once in your shoes for their advice and the smartest choices they made.

HOW TO ENCOURAGE FRIENDS WHO
LOSE THEIR JOB

+ Just listen! Don't be a fortune-teller or go into a dissertation about your uncle Bob's being out of work for four years.
+ Offer to help your friends make a list of contacts, agencies, and other resources that can be of use. Also offer to help rejuvenate their résumé, or show them the ropes on social media if they haven't yet taken a plunge in that direction.
+ Call in and check on them once a week, meet them for coffee, and again just listen. Try to have positive news or something of interest to say or show them, maybe a favorite magazine with an article about their favorite sports figure or designer.
+ Get tickets to a sporting event, movie, or play and treat them to an evening out. You can make it as simple or special as they will allow, without making them feel uncomfortable.
+ Send a positive e-mail or two a week, sending links to articles of interest that are uplifting.
+ Don't smother them by trying to act as their personal "get a new job" ambassador.

FUNERALS

Funerals can cause a lapse of judgment in the verbal and reasoning skills of many otherwise articulate individuals. Dealing with the loss of a loved one or friends who have lost a loved one is awkward for most and mystifying for many. People wring their hands wondering what they should say and do.

There are just *two* things to keep in mind.

+ Be there! You must show up.
+ Be brief in what you say.

The worst response is to do nothing at all, or to avoid the people who are grieving out of fear of saying or doing the wrong

thing. Yes, it's highly uncomfortable to all involved, but the people who have lost a loved one need support and comforting.

Below are a few ways to navigate a funeral and bereavement.

+ Do something (anything) but just remember that doing nothing is not an option.
+ Never, ever launch into your own sad story of losing a loved one.
+ Do not say, "I know how you feel," or forecast how they will feel in the future, chanting things like "Time heals all wounds" or "A day doesn't go by that I don't think about my sweet Ralph and wish he were here, and he's been dead thirty years." How is that going to help anyone?
+ At times like these we all could benefit from a little extra help: "I'm here for you."

- Mention that you're an early bird or a night owl and can be called anytime.
- Try your best to keep your comments brief, saying, "I am thinking of you and your family." That's it, plain and simple.
- If it's culturally acceptable, a hug says a lot.

WAYS TO HELP BEFORE THE FUNERAL

- Think of what needs to be done and offer to help by making suggestions. Call and say, "I will pick up Maggie at school for you. I could bring her home or keep her for a play date so you will have more time to attend to things." You could also say, "I will be dropping off dinner when dropping off Maggie," and just like that you've helped in two ways. You provided a solution for child care and dinner.
- Never call and say, "What can I do?" People grieving are sometimes in shock, and it unfairly puts the burden on them to help you think of something to do. Instead, always offer a solution or way you might help.
- Ask if you can help call other friends and family members to share the news of the passing.
- See if help is needed with the funeral arrangements, or send a plant or flowers that say, "Thinking of you." If the family have stated they prefer donations be made in the name of the deceased in lieu of flowers, follow their wishes.
- Be sure to post your online memorial to be read by the loved ones after all the funeral rituals have ended.
- If the ceremony is private, they still need to hear from you and be comforted.

WAYS TO HELP DURING THE FUNERAL

- Sign the guest register.
- Be brief in your condolences.
- Think of a way to help and do it.
- Arrive at the funeral on time. If you are late, slip in a side door and take a seat at a side pew.

- Wearing black and gray aren't required anymore, but they are a safe bet. You can wear other colors as long as they are conservative. It's not the time to break out your leopard or zebra shirt and green golf pants.
- Leave your phone in the car so there's no temptation to text, or (worse) possibility that the phone will ring.

WAYS TO HELP AFTER THE FUNERAL

- Help address thank-you notes and/or write them on behalf of the grieving individual.
- Clean the closets and take things to a charitable organization.
- Help return the dishes from meals that were brought over.
- Assist with child care, as the person is still grieving and coming out of shock.
- If you are good at putting things in order, help go through the legalities and assist in getting paperwork in order for the attorneys.
- Ask if the person needs help choosing the grave marker, and make sure it's in place within the year.
- Write a note or letter about all the good memories you have of the person who passed and send it to their loved ones as a treasured memory.
- Don't forget about the grieving person. Make a reminder on your calendar to touch base monthly. A phone call, short note, lunch, or coffee meeting would be a nice gesture. Don't say, "Would you like to go to lunch?" Say, "I would like to take you to lunch. Is Tuesday or Thursday at noon good for you?"

CELEBRATION-OF-LIFE CEREMONIES

- If the deceased will be laid to rest in a celebration of life, such as a tree planting where everyone wears jeans, or a Parrothead Jimmy Buffett celebration where everyone wears Hawaiian shirts, go with the wishes of the family. Don't judge; honor the person who has passed with their last wish.

ILLNESS / UNFAVORABLE
MEDICAL DIAGNOSIS

If someone shares with you that they or a loved one has a life-threatening disease, you should listen to them closely and completely. Once they have finished, offer a reply and share your thoughts and compassion.

- ✦ Tell them you are thinking of them and suggest ways you would like to help. Be specific: ask if you can bring dinner over, take them to appointments, care for the kids, mow the lawn, etc.
- ✦ Be careful not to launch into an awkward diatribe because you are uncomfortable and don't know what to say. Example: "My uncle Paul on my mother's side had the same illness and he was never quite the same."
- ✦ Don't ask probing medical questions or inquire if their life insurance is up-to-date.
- ✦ Come together with a few friends and coordinate visits and responsibilities, such as delivering food, shopping, responding to e-mails or handwritten communications, even helping with writing out their bills.
- ✦ Sending them personalized cheerful or humorous cards will help lift their spirits.
- ✦ Bring over books on tape, or if they love cooking, send videos on food preparation. Tailor the distraction to their interests.
- ✦ If they have a caretaker, offer to sit with the patient so the caretaker can get some rest and regroup.
- ✦ Never say, "I know how you feel," because even if you do, it doesn't make them feel any better.
- ✦ Sometimes a heartfelt hug or sincere touch magically translates into how much you care . . . no words are needed.

Fourteen

CELEBRATIONS

We Are Family! Aren't We?

Celebrations typically have one thing in common: they gather people who are related in some way, toasting a glorious event. When we come together to celebrate, our loved ones and extended loved ones are usually there for us to usher in the festivity. But families are also the people who drive us the craziest! Having a few plans for the celebration will ensure that it will be exactly what it's supposed to be: family and friends coming together to honor rites of passage and achievement.

Go to the celebration intending to honor the person being celebrated. Ask how you can be of help. When Uncle Henry Walker, the close talker, gets you in his grip, listen to him even if he is telling you about his bravado in World War II. When Aunt Gertie with her fragrant breath holds you close in a taloned grasp, hold your breath and hug her right back. Engage with the children attending the celebration, as they are full of wonder and give the heart an extra beat. As you cut the cake, dance the dances, and sing the songs, look around: all these characters are your special family and make distinctive deposits in your heart.

ANNIVERSARIES

Every time a wedding anniversary is observed, it is like a renewal of the couple's commitment to each other and deserves to be celebrated in a memorable way. Family members or close friends may want to throw an anniversary party for the milestone years, and the best way to honor the occasion is to put the couple's desires first and foremost.

Here are some ideas to help you plan an anniversary celebration.

- ✦ If you are considering a surprise party for the couple, gather a small committee who will help organize and facilitate the event while also keeping it under wraps.
- ✦ If you are renting a space for the occasion, you will want to secure the venue roughly six months to a year in advance.
- ✦ Send out the invitations about four to six weeks before the anniversary party and perhaps a "save the date" notice if you have several people coming from out of state.
- ✦ The party can be anything from simple to extravagant, including the décor, music, and food of your choice. You will want to include a guest book for everyone to sign and leave sentiments as a keepsake for the couple. You can include a wedding photo of the honored guests and a scrapbook of their lives together. Also, ask their friends if they have any photographs of the couple and make a display for all to enjoy.
- ✦ Commonly, the oldest son will sit to the right of his mother, and the oldest daughter will sit to her father's left. Also, the best man and maid of honor sit with their spouses at the head table.
- ✦ If you are giving a toast, be sure to share stories about both husband and wife, as the celebration is about them as a couple. Invite others to share as well.
- ✦ If a close family member or friend is hosting the anniversary party, it is proper for them to pay for everyone present.

BRIDAL AND BABY SHOWERS
The Bridal Shower

Bridal showers honor an engaged couple with a celebration that includes guests who are close to the couple, sharing a meal, and gifts that help get the new couple started in their lives together. Here are a few tips about the protocol of a bridal shower.

- Close friends of the bride-to-be generally host a bridal shower. They choose the venue, arrange for the food and cake, and send out the shower invitations.
- The shower should take place four to eight weeks before the wedding, and invitations should be sent three to five weeks before the shower.
- Invitations ought to include the guest of honor's name, and the groom's name if it's a couple's shower. Include the date, time, address, and the host's name, phone number, e-mail address, and an RSVP date. If it's a couple's shower, note that on the invitation.
- Directions, a map, wedding registry, theme, and wedding Web site information can be included on a separate sheet of paper and inserted in the envelope with the invitation, but never written on it.
- Make sure whoever receives an invitation to a shower is also on the wedding guest list. If the bride is having several showers, be sure that no one is invited to more than one unless it's a close family member or bridesmaid. If a person is invited to more than one shower, then a gift is given only at the first one.
- Couple's showers have become popular and follow the same protocol as a shower historically given for the bride.
- The bride-to-be (or couple) should be prompt with their thank-you notes, sending them to all the attendees and anyone else who sent a gift. The host should receive a gift from the bride- and groom-to-be and a thoughtful note of thanks.

The Baby Shower

A baby shower is a wonderful celebration held for an expectant mom (and sometimes dad, too) before the baby arrives. It is a fun and special way to help out the parents-to-be with items they will need for their new little bundle of joy.

Here are a few tips for either planning or attending a baby shower.

+ Invitations should be sent out three to four weeks prior to the shower. It's best to have the shower at least two months

before the baby's due date, or you may end up having an extraspecial little guest attending the shower.

+ The invitation should include the guest of honor's name(s), the mother (and father, if he is attending). Also, the date and time of the shower, address and map of location, the host's name, phone number, e-mail, the RSVP date, and the sex of the baby if known.

+ When your guests arrive, greet them at the door, introduce them to other attendees, and show them where the food and drinks are. A baby shower usually lasts about two hours, so keep it going by making sure the guests are eating, meeting new people, and enjoying those they already know.

+ Keep games to a minimum of two or three at the most. The gift opening should be the highlight of the entertainment. Keep the gift opening moving forward by making sure you have helpers to hand over the gifts and then remove the unwrapped paper. Another assistant can record the gift giver's name and gift, to make it easier on the guest of honor, who will want to write a proper thank-you later.

+ If it's a first-time mother, be careful about what you say. Never ask how much weight she has gained. If she asks you about your experience while having your child, refrain from telling her it was a personal Vietnam, even if it was. There is no need to send her into early labor by frightening her.

+ Be careful not to launch into a lecture on parenting tips and advice: it could overwhelm the expectant parents.

+ If this is a second child, a kind gesture is to bring a little something for the big brother- or sister-to-be.

+ A nice touch for the expectant parents is to enclose an index card with the invitation asking each invitee to write their favorite parenting tip, or favorite memory of being a parent. This can be sent back in the RSVP envelope or brought to the shower.

+ Remember to honor the expectant grandmother with a

corsage. Have her tell a few favorite memories from when she had her daughter or son.

+ Before you leave, be sure to ask if you can help with anything, thank the host for the invitation, and say good-bye to everyone.

+ The expectant mom and dad should write those thank-you notes ASAP, so all the lovely guests who attended their shower will be properly acknowledged. Don't wait, because you may become overwhelmed once your baby arrives and with thanking friends and family for the gifts you received while in the hospital.

GRADUATIONS

A high school or college graduation celebration is an important commemoration in young people's lives. Although the grads may not be into all the pomp and circumstance, celebrating this mile-stone in their lives with family and friends is exciting, as they look back on what they have accomplished and look forward to what the world has to offer.

Here are some tips to help you prepare for graduation with confidence.

HOST DUTIES

+ Students are allowed only so many tickets to their graduation ceremony since most schools have limited seating. Fortunately, most people understand you are limited. If you have a graduation party afterward, then the guest list can be extended to more relatives and friends.

+ Send friends and family who will not be able to attend the graduation events an announcement.

+ If you have received graduation gifts, you must send a handwritten thank-you note for each gift. Do this as soon as possible, preferably within the first week of receiving the gift. The notes don't have to be lengthy, but be sure to thank the guests for attending the ceremony or the party, thank them for the gift they gave or sent, and mention how much their thoughtfulness means to you.

GUEST DUTIES

✦ We all know graduation ceremonies can be lengthy, but avoid the temptation to skip out after your graduate receives their diploma. Be considerate of the grads who are at the end of the alphabet. They will appreciate being cheered on as well.

✦ Be sure you don't use your cell phone during the ceremony. If you have a call you just cannot put on hold, make sure your phone is on vibrate and then leave the ceremony during your conversation. Keep it brief so you can get back. Remember, no texting.

✦ You are not obligated to give a gift just because you received a graduation invitation or announcement. If you choose to, the most important thing is to give what you can afford. Sometimes a personal gift is the most treasured, such as an album of photos of you and the grad together through the years, or a treasured book new or old, or a signed first-edition book.

RELIGIOUS BIRTH AND COMING-OF-AGE CEREMONIES

Baptisms and Christenings

In Christianity, baptisms and christenings are slightly different, yet both are ceremonies of initiation into the faith. They are important occasions to both family and friends and are typically followed by a celebration.

✦ Godparents are chosen by the parents of the child. They are to play an important spiritual role in the life of the child, taking a special interest in the child's religious

upbringing. At the baptism or christening, they may want
to present the child with a special gift.

+ The child will wear a nice white outfit, and guests should
dress in proper church attire.
+ Since family and friends generally attend the service, it is
common to have a party immediately following. The
parents may choose to invite a small, intimate group of
close family and friends or turn it into a larger gathering.
+ Invitations should be mailed six to eight weeks before the
event.

Bris

A bris is the Jewish rite of circumcision, which represents a newborn boy's relationship with God and his Jewish heritage. During
this ceremony, the child will receive his Hebrew name.

+ Parents may choose to celebrate afterward with a casual meal.
Close family and friends are generally invited to attend.
+ Guests will want to offer a small gift to honor the child.

Aqiqah

In this Muslim ritual, performed on the seventh or twenty-first
day after birth, a newborn's hair is shaved off to signify a new
phase of life outside the womb.

+ The family celebrates with relatives and friends with a feast
of thanksgiving. The gathering is usually held in a social
hall at a mosque and will include goat or lamb.
+ Guests generally bring a gift for the child.

First Communion

First Communion is a Christian ceremony in which a child receives for the first time the bread and wine known as the host.

This important spiritual event for the child is celebrated with their family and friends.

Customs vary based on the religious affiliation, but following are some general guidelines when celebrating with the child.

- If you attend the ceremony, follow the denominational rules as to whether you receive Communion with the child and the rest of the congregation.
- If you are a guest, wear regular Sunday church attire.
- Parents may host a party after the Communion service. This is generally held at their home or a restaurant. Close family and friends of the child are generally invited.
- Guests may want to bring a gift for the child, perhaps something of a spiritual nature. Some ideas: a Bible or prayer book, across necklace or pendant, a card that honors the occasion.

Confirmation

In some Christian denominations, at a certain age young people celebrate their confirmation, which is a rite of initiation for the purpose of bestowing the gifts of the Holy Spirit. Some families may host a party after the church service and will invite relatives and close friends.

Here are some guidelines when attending a confirmation party.

- The invitation will guide you on whether the event is formal or casual. If you are unsure of what to wear, always err on the side of being overdressed rather than under.
- You may want to bring a gift for the confirmation guest of honor. Be sure to congratulate them and thank the host for inviting you.
- The honoree should thank people for their gifts with a handwritten note within two to three weeks after the celebration.

Bar/Bat Mitzvah

The bar mitzvah and bat mitzvah are comparable to the Christian confirmation. This celebration occurs when a Jewish boy turns thirteen or a Jewish girl turns twelve. It is a celebration of the young person's being accepted as an adult member of their congregation.

Following are some tips if you are invited to a bar/bat mitzvah.

+ Families often celebrate this important occasion in their child's life by holding a formal reception and inviting relatives and friends. It may be a sit-down dinner or buffet style, held at their home or at a restaurant.
+ Let the invitation be your guide as to how formal the event will be.
+ It is customary to honor the young adult with a special gift. Some ideas: a Star of David pendant, savings bond, gift certificate, or book on Jewish history.
+ Be sure to congratulate the honoree when you arrive at the reception.
+ The honoree should send handwritten thank-you notes for their gifts within two to three weeks of the celebration.

QUINCEAÑERAS AND SWEET SIXTEENS

Quinceañera

Quinceañera is a Latino celebration that honors a young lady's fifteenth birthday. It is considered the transition from childhood to adulthood. The event can include a religious ceremony followed by a party, or a party may take place without the ceremony. Here are some tips for participating in this special celebration.

+ The festivity could be a simple get-together with friends and family, or an elaborate black-tie affair with the guest of honor wearing a formal gown. The invitation will announce whether it is formal or casual.

* Gifts are part of the event but never mentioned in the invitation. Traditionally, gifts should not be opened during the event. A few gift ideas would be a cross, a rosary, or a picture frame engraved with the date of the quinceañera.
* Thank-you notes for all gifts should be handwritten and sent within two or three weeks of the celebration.

Sweet Sixteen Birthday Party

Sweet sixteen celebrations, which originated in the United States, signify a young lady going from childhood to adulthood. The event can be formal or an informal barbecue or pizza party. Whichever way the guest of honor decides to celebrate, keep a few rules in mind.

* Find the guest of honor upon arrival and congratulate her. Try to be understanding if she only spends a few minutes with you, as she needs to talk to many guests during the celebration.
* Whatever the family customs are, follow and honor them by participating. Be positive, upbeat, and mingle, and you will be a great addition to the party.
* When it's time to leave, the best way to make a graceful exit is to find the host and the guest of honor and thank them for having you as a part of such a special celebration. Also mention something you enjoyed, such as the music, food, etc.
* Thank-you notes for all gifts should be handwritten and sent within two or three weeks of the celebration.

WEDDINGS

When a wedding invitation arrives, RSVP as soon as possible. Check your calendar to see if the date is open and respond immediately!

If you can attend, keep a copy of the invitation on the fridge or bulletin board. On the day of the big event, you can readily access it for time and location.

Below are some more tips to ensure you are the perfect wedding guest.

- ✦ Don't edit the invitation. If your name is riding on the envelope solo, that means just you, not your cousin, Mama, or the guy you just met at the Maroon 5 concert. The couple may be working with a tight budget or space restrictions.
- ✦ Arrive on time. This isn't the occasion to be "fashionably late." The rule of thumb is to arrive fifteen minutes early, and if it is a larger wedding of two hundred or more people, arrive thirty minutes early.
- ✦ Don't be a Peeping Tom. If you do arrive late, wait until the bride has walked down the aisle before you take your seat. No looking through the crack of the closed doors.
- ✦ The music was arranged a year in advance, so your techno-funk ringtone isn't a welcome part of the arrangement. Leave your smartphone in the car. The ceremony will only be an hour, so have the decency, respect, and willpower to disconnect!
- ✦ Leave your junk in the trunk. This is not the day to talk about your latest breakup or mole removal. It's a day to celebrate all things beautiful and new. Keep your conversations positive and upbeat.
- ✦ Shake your groove thing. If the deejay or band breaks out with *Soul Train* sounds, jump in and do those moves that you've been practicing in your living room for the past twenty years. Be a part of the celebration and mingle, mingle, mingle. Be sure you don't latch onto the same people you've known your whole life. Dance, sign the guest book, enjoy the food, and catch the bouquet or the garter. Be a fun part of the magical day.
- ✦ What to wear? White is not an option! You can't wear

white, bone, or beige to the wedding. It's taboo! You have a plethora of colors to choose from, so reconnect with your color wheel.

+ Don't be a stalker. If you have questions about the wedding, please don't call the bride and groom. Ask their parents or siblings, or, better yet, see if they have a wedding Web site. The site can answer all your questions. Noteworthy: it is best to mail your gift to the couple's home address for a safe delivery.

◆ A kind gesture. The professional photographer won't have the wedding pictures ready for almost a month. Send the photos that you snapped to the newlyweds a day or two after the wedding. The pictures will be a nice surprise for the honeymooners upon their return, and just like that you've provided an unanticipated treasure for them to enjoy.

Questions and Answers

Q: *I was out to eat with my aunt and about to take a bite of my chicken marsala when she said, "Dear, you've put on weight." I just paused, as I didn't know if I was more confused by her breach of etiquette or that maybe I had gained a few pounds. Her statement made the rest of our elegant lunch awkward and unappetizing. We both weaved through the rest of the meal not mentioning the change of atmosphere. How should I have reacted to that statement?*

A: Maybe your aunt had a lapse in manners or is getting Alzheimer's. Here is the rule I think is safe to keep on your social tool belt—if it can't be remedied or corrected in three minutes, never mention it. Parsley in your teeth, a hair hitching a ride on your sweater, or an unzipped zipper are all fine to call to someone's attention and notice would be appreciated by the recipient. The weight statement is 100 percent off-limits since it can't be corrected in three minutes. This also goes for statements about someone's physical features—nose size, frizzy hair, eye bags, acne, height, etc.

Q: *I don't know how to say no. My friend is always asking me to volunteer for all the committees she has decided to chair. I don't support the same causes and would rather be with my family or donate that time to my church. How do I say no without seeming rude and unhelpful? No matter what I say, she has a comeback and I usually end up helping her.*

A: It's easy to escape your caped volunteer crusader's quest to pull you on board. You only need to say no with respect and graciousness. I learned this from my friend Bob Burg. He suggests you make a point of lavishing appreciation for the "offer" while declining. Example: "Thank you so much. I'm honored to even be thought of in that way—that you would think highly enough of me to ask me to serve on this committee. While I choose not to take that on, I really appreciate your kind offer." The key is to not give an excuse or reason. Doing so would give the person something tangible to answer, and that can trip you up. If you say, "I don't have time" or "I don't have the skill" or something similar, the person can then answer the objection, which forces you to either come up with another one, accept the task, or admit that you were fibbing.

Q: I am new to Facebook and was wondering how to exhibit the proper social skills in online communication. Below are my questions.

(a) What is the protocol for instant-message "chatting" if you see someone, a friend, online?

A: You can't tell what he or she might be doing, so saying something like "Hey, love to catch up when you get a chance" leaves it open for them to respond.

(b) How do I respond to unwanted cause requests? What is the best way to tell them nicely that I'm not interested in joining their cause?

A: It depends on how well you know the person. You could say, "Gee, I'd love to but I'm already committed to my own causes, wishing you the best."

(c) How do I say no to a Friend request?

A: Simply click Ignore, no explanation is needed.

(d) What is the best way to unfriend someone?

A: Just unfriend, they don't get a notification. And if they come back to you, you can simply share that you are limiting your account to friends and family with whom you have real-world relationships, not simply virtual (or whatever you want to say).

Q: My neighbor often says, "You look tired." It's always when I feel great. I usually retort, "I'm fine" or "Yeah, it's been a long week," when I really want to say, "You look unmannerly," but that would be unmannerly. What should I say?

A: Not one good thing can come out of a statement such as that. No response is needed, as it's not your job to teach other folks etiquette or respond to their feigned displays of concern. Just ignore the statement, change the subject, or ask a question to steer the conversation elsewhere.

Q: My cousin is always pushing his political agenda onto our fun family dinner parties and outings. I don't agree with his stances or politics. How do I steer clear of these statements and diatribes without appearing rude?

A: You don't need to give an opinion. You could just answer, "That is interesting," or repeat back what the person is saying: "Oh, you feel that the ban on chicken farming is a conspiracy?" and with that your cousin feels heard. Next, change the subject by asking a question. We are thinking of getting a cabin for the kids during spring break. Do you know the best way to go about doing that? Is it costly? Do you think the kids will enjoy it? It's that simple—you've moved the conversation to a fun topic.

Q: My neighbor's children walk in my house without knocking and open my fridge and pantry without asking. What should I do or say?

A: I would walk the children back to the door and ask, "What should you do when you are visiting someone's home?" I would show them how to knock and also ring the doorbell. Remind them to knock or ring only once while waiting for a response. This is best done in question form so it's an interactive dialogue. Example: "How many times do you think we should ring the bell or knock?" I would then explain that if they are hungry or thirsty, they could ask a parent for a drink or something to eat, as opposed to just helping themselves. I would also role-play with this child. The goal is to teach with love and compassion, not shame and frustration. If the child doesn't have proper boundaries already set, then gently teaching the child will help them wherever they go, not just in your house. Just like that, in about three minutes you've taught social skills to a child that will serve them for a lifetime.

Q: My daughter is getting ready to graduate from college. Could you give me three tips that will help her in interviews?

A: Three skills that will make you stand out throughout your entire life are: (1) Have a strong handshake as well as body language. Stand tall and erect, and walk with a purpose. (2) Remember other people's names. If you can hone and perfect that skill, doors will be opened that would normally remain shut. (3) Write thank-you notes for everything. For each and every interview you go on, thank the interviewer and also the receptionist. Thank your doctors, trash collectors, etc. Make a habit of writing three thank-you notes a week. Three to four lines takes about three minutes. Send notes within three days of what you are acknowledging. This one habit will not only enrich your life, but also the lives of others.

Q: I was with a client at lunch last week and my boss came into the restaurant. I didn't know whom to introduce first.

A: This is a common dilemma, as so many rules govern an introduction. I have an easy and fail-safe way to remember how to make a proper introduction. The most important person's name is said first. The client, in this circumstance, is the most important person. Example: (Client) "Dee Akhavein, I would like to introduce to you Jayanne Roggenbaum, our chief executive officer." You've honored the client and made the perfect introduction.

Q: I was out to dinner with people from the law firm I work for when I accidentally used one of the partners' bread plate. He said I needed an etiquette class. I was mortified. Do you have an easy method to remember how to locate my bread plate when the table is crowded with china, crystal, and silverware?

A: I would say that the partner is the one in need of an etiquette class. Mistakenly using another person's bread plate is a common error and should never have been mentioned in front of your colleagues. The number-one rule of protocol, etiquette, and manners is to always put other people at ease, which the partner truly didn't do. He should have opted to use the left side of his entrée plate and then shared his concern out of the public eye. I remember how to locate my bread plate by thinking BMW—bread-meal-water, from left to right. This will help you remember where your drink is located as well.

Q: I feel awkward in social situations, especially if the people I am around are more educated, attractive, and worldly than I am. Do you have any advice about how to feel more at ease in social situations?

A: First of all, you aren't alone. Ninety percent of my clients, whether they are athletes, entertainers, business professionals, recent college graduates, or everyday moms and dads, hope that I can help them with networking skills and being more at ease in public. Here are three tips to help you during your next networking event, party, or social function: (1) Since you are aware that many people share your social concerns, go with the aim of making someone else feel at ease. When you are getting dressed, driving to the event, and walking up to the door, say to yourself, *I am going to talk to someone else who feels exactly like I do and make them feel at ease.* Then the pressure is off you. (2) Think about your latest trip, something you learned, or something funny that would be of interest to others. Also, read the Internet for the latest business news and be prepared to talk about it. (3) People love to answer questions about themselves, so have open-ended questions ready to ask. You could inquire where their favorite vacation was and what made it so neat. If they build sailboats, ask them how they got into the sailboat-making business. People love to share things about their lives. Be careful not to interrogate folks or seem as if you are interviewing them, and, as I said, have some of these same points of interest to share about yourself. If you are a reading teacher and people ask what you do, you could say, "I prepare children and adults to travel, grow, and soar, all for the mere cost of a book."